WESSELHOEFT
Traded to the Enemy

WESSELHOEFT
Traded to the Enemy

A six-year-old American child interned
and then exchanged with our enemy to
endure bombing, deprivation and fear

*To
Anita Bowen
May god bless America
Adolf W Wesselhoeft
Lt Col USAF Ret
6/5/21*

The Story of Adolf "Wes" Wesselhoeft
as told to Shirley Anderson Wesselhoeft

Remember D-day 6/6

FIRST U.S. PRINT EDITION
    Paperback   ISBN-13: 978-1725055919
                ISBN-10: 1725055910
    Hardback   ISBN-13: 978-1-945333-14-9
                ISBN-10: 1-945333-14-6

Available from Amazon.com and other book stores

Printed in U.S.A.

To contact author with feedback, or for speaking engagements or book club purchases, please email us at ajwesselhoeft@hotmail.com
318–254–1166

Dedication

This book is dedicated to all the children who, although American citizens like me, were exchanged with our enemy and sent into an active war zone. The only satisfaction that I feel from this ill-fated trade is in knowing it resulted in the return of wounded warriors and the other fellow Americans for whom we were exchanged.

I also hope this book honors my parents who immigrated to America and were interned without due process as "enemy aliens" during World War II. Despite this, they raised me to love America and encouraged me to return and serve this great country.

The LORD is my shepherd; I shall not want.

He maketh me to lie down in green pastures: he leadeth me beside the still waters.

He restoreth my soul: he leadeth me in the paths of righteousness for his name's sake.

Yea, though I walk through the valley of the shadow of death, I will fear no evil: for thou art with me; thy rod and thy staff they comfort me.

Thou preparest a table before me in the presence of mine enemies: thou anointest my head with oil; my cup runneth over.

Surely goodness and mercy shall follow me all the days of my life: and I will dwell in the house of the LORD for ever.

Psalm 23:1-6 KJV

Acknowledgements

We are especially grateful to the Texas Historical Commission (THC) for their diligent research into the history of Crystal City Family Internment Camp, Crystal City, Texas. Their work has helped preserve the history of the camp and its internees—German Americans, Italian Americans, Japanese Americans as well as people of those ancestries from Latin America.

They have also brought to light the disturbing fact that internees, including American citizens, were held there until they could be exchanged on board the *SS Gripsholm* for American detainees held by our enemy.

They made sure that signage around the camp tells the full story and have produced beautiful, thorough brochures about the internment camps in Texas that are available to the public.

The prestige of the Texas Historical Commission has been of tremendous value to us as we talk to people who have never heard of German American internment. Additionally, we thank Dr. Lila Rakoczy, who has taken Wes' oral history, helped us to research German American internment, and connected us with other people interested in World War II internment.

We are thankful for the enthusiastic support we have received from the Chennault Aviation and

Military Museum, Monroe, Louisiana. President and CEO Nell Chennault Calloway, granddaughter of the famous Flying Tiger, General Claire Chennault, immediately grasped the significance of this story and placed a display on the events in the museum, including a video of Wes' oral history. Her very talented staff, including Roy Bullock, Gary Vieaux and Bob Jackson, have been supportive and have lent their many talents to telling our story. We consider them all to be our friends.

The National Archives at Washington, DC, and College Park, Maryland, and staff have been very helpful in our research, which we hope to continue.

The University of Texas, San Antonio, and Virginia Wood Davis Archives of Southwest Texas, Uvalde, Texas, have provided pictures for this book from their special collections. We are grateful to them for their cooperation and help.

Our 75th Anniversary Commemoration was a memorable event to us especially because of the support and participation of family, friends, local authorities and fellow veterans. We especially thank Crystal City Mayor Frank Moreno Jr. and his staff. Thank you to the American Legion Melecio Ortiz Post 296, especially Mr. George Rodriquez, Adjutant, and the Color Guard. We also thank Crystal City Independent School District. Thank you to Debbie Galerneau. We made many new friends in the local area and continue to be in contact with them.

We thank Barb Evenson and her staff, Mimi Lancsak, Bonnie Norrod and Adam Grigg, and volunteers Chris Bull and Anton Kaiser, for diligent editing and photo work which improved this book significantly.

We are blessed beyond measure with a loving family and friends who have been supportive of us as we have commemorated, traveled and written this book, most of all Scott and Riley Harrison; and Heather, Mitch, Lauren, Maryanna, Mitchell and Landon Spillers. We are so grateful to Heather for all the hours of work she put in proofreading and even editing this book. Also we are thankful to Alton and Ronnie Spillers who have been so supportive. We could not have done it without all your help and love.

For our Nealy we offer a special pat on the head and a few extra treats. He rode quietly many miles in the car and guided us safely while on foot.

We especially thank all the wonderful American people we met as we traveled. So many were helpful with information, expressed gratitude to Wes for his service, and enthusiastically encouraged us to write and publish this book. Most importantly they became friends. They have contributed significantly to our memories.

Wes and Shirley

Special thanks

Most of all I thank my wife, Shirley, for the
countless hours, days and nights she has
spent writing this book. Without her this book
would not have been written. She has patient-
ly helped me express what I want to say and
diligently corrected errors that kept slipping
in. I am very thankful for her understanding
of military life and German culture which has
made telling this story with her so much easier
and more meaningful to me. She has unself-
ishly put a moratorium on her own passions
such as sewing in order to do research, drive
me long distances, send innumerable emails
and make many phone calls. Her contribu-
tion is truly an expression of love for me and
of our great country. Thank you, Shirley.
Your loving husband, Wes

Contents

PART TWO

Foreword

As the head of the Chennault Aviation & Military Museum I have had the privilege of meeting countless heroes. I have been blessed to talk to many great people who have sacrificed more than most of us can imagine to give us the great lives we all enjoy today. Many of them have lived, and still live, with the horrors of war. I have never served in the armed forces, so all I can do is try to serve those who have.

A little over a year ago, we held the Military Officers luncheon at the Museum, which we have on several occasions. As I was welcoming the group, I noticed that one of the visitors had a beautiful black dog and assumed it was a service dog. After the lunch, I introduced myself to Shirley and Wes Wesselhoeft and asked about their dog. I was told that it was a guide dog because Wes had been exposed to Agent Orange during his time in Vietnam and was legally blind because of it. It always breaks my heart to hear how our veterans have suffered because of their service to our country; however, this was only the beginning of his story.

I soon learned an incredible story about a very young boy, an American citizen, who had been placed

Nell Chennault Calloway with Wesselhoeft exhibit at the Chennault Aviation & Military Museum, Monroe, Louisiana.

Exhibit includes a taped interview with Wes, photos of the Crystal City Family Internment Camp where Wes and his family were interned, a model of the ship he took back to the United States, medals from his 22-year U.S. Air Force career, and other items. Photo used by permission of Chennault Museum.

in an internment camp at the age of 6. He and his parents were living an idyllic American dream in Chicago, Illinois, but due to his parents' German citizenship, during World War II the family was sent to an internment camp in Crystal City, Texas. They were then sent to Germany and exchanged for other American citizens.

They lived in Hamburg, Germany, during the war where they were bombed by the Americans during the day and by the British at night. What impressed me the most was that while he was telling the story there was no bitterness in his voice. I was also impressed that even after suffering such terrible treatment by the United States government, as a young man he still found a way to come back to the United States. After arriving back home, one of the first things he did was sign up to serve our country, the same country that had given him away. After hearing his story, I knew that we needed to tell it here at the Museum. We are blessed to have an exhibit based on documented facts and his recorded history during this very difficult time.

Wes' story is an inspirational account of a true American hero. This is the story of a young boy cruelly uprooted from a normal life. He was sent to a war zone and not only survived the war but also a very harsh life in post-war Germany. He somehow managed to survive with his faith, dignity and a sense of humanity intact.

I feel very honored and humbled to know him and to even try to express my admiration for him is incredibly difficult to put in words. I can only hope that people will read this book and know that it is possible to overcome great adversity and still be an American Hero.

Nell Chennault Calloway
CEO, Chennault Aviation & Military Museum
Monroe, Louisiana

Preface

We have been on a magnificent journey together while writing this book and commemorating the 75th Anniversary of Wes' internment in Crystal City, Texas. We have spent many hours talking over details of his experience.

Together we came to realize that there were so many things we had never discussed. Even though we had talked many times about the topic in general, it is hard to imagine that somehow we have been together all these years and yet there was so much untold, unspoken between us. There were so many events to describe and to come to understand.

We decided to write this book because so little is known in our country about German internment and we hoped that by telling this story others would know and understand our American history. We also hope that German internment will eventually be recognized by our government as have been the internment of Japanese and Italian Americans.

Simply telling his story as Wes remembers it seemed to be the right approach. Any research we have done for this book has been solely to obtain pictures so it could be better understood. We did not want to go into the very complicated historical and political aspects of World War II internment. He does not know those things firsthand or in detail but he does remember what happened to him and his family. These facts are indisputable.

Our decision was to include some important information about his military service because we feel it is so relevant to the story. After all, he not only served this great country for twenty-two years but he is legally blind due to his exposure to Agent Orange while serving in Vietnam.

Wes also wanted to share his spiritual journey from his innocent belief in God as a child to his becoming a Christian man. This is at least something that we had discussed in depth and we both understood fully before undertaking writing the book.

PART ONE

CHAPTER 1

New York City, USA!

New York, February 1958. I could hardly believe it! After ten days at sea, enduring seasickness in the belly of a steel monster steaming across the North Atlantic, I was finally here!

Now age twenty-one, I left Germany with $20, a camera, a guitar, and a few clothes in a leather suitcase my father had given me. I had no idea what I would be doing in America, where I would go, or what would happen to me.

I spent most of the first five days of the voyage in "Stateroom 245," an inexpensive room in the very bottom of the *SS Ryndam*. Occasionally, someone from the ship's crew came by and gave me saltines. These did not stop the sickness in any way, but it did give my body something to expel from my otherwise empty stomach.

At times I felt a bit better and thought that if I went upstairs out into the fresh air perhaps that would help. But instead most of the time I ended up leaning over the rails trying to rid my stomach of its non-existent contents.

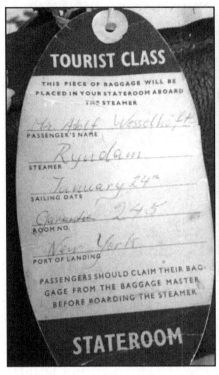

Luggage tags on Wes' guitar on return trip to the US on the Holland America Line ship *SS Ryndam*

Gradually I felt better and began eating small amounts. The food on board was excellent, very plentiful and beautifully presented. By the last day before arriving in New York, I was well enough to enjoy the seven-course dinners, huge breakfasts, and delicious snacks that were always available.

As the steamer *Ryndam* slowly made its way through New York Harbor, everyone hurried to the side of the ship. For many passengers this would be their first glimpse of the Statue of Liberty. I wondered if the ship was listing due to all the passengers gathered on the ship's side rails. They shouted and waved with great excitement and energy. As for me, I quietly held my Kodak camera and took pictures of the Statue of Liberty, the very symbol of America and the freedom it promises. She was indisputable proof that after enduring war, deprivation, fear, ruin, and uncertainty I had finally arrived in New York Harbor and was once again in America.

Early in the afternoon of February 3, 1958, the *Ryndam* docked at the Fifth Street Pier in New Jersey. The other passengers and I disembarked into the bitter cold and wind. We were instructed to queue up according to our entrance status, such as citizen, immigrant, tourist, etc. I, of course, stood in the citizen line, looking around to see if I recognized any of the people I met on board.

The Holland America Line apparently had made hotel arrangements for us which included bus transportation. The cost of this for me was $10, half of all I had to my name.

As we left the bleak, industrialized area of the wharf and turned onto Times Square, the city suddenly burst into light. Every square inch seemed covered with billboards. Each of the billboards was lit up with neon lights and many had lights which formed words that ran across the board. I could not make any sense of them and there were so many that as the bus moved along I was not able to watch an entire message. They seemed to be incomplete sentences like headlines, advertisement messages, or ticker tapes. It was such an amazing sight, unlike anything I had seen in fourteen years in Germany.

With so many new, fascinating sights and stimulations, I just stared out of the window trying to absorb all I was seeing and hearing of New York City. The honking of car horns, sounds of moving traffic, and ordinary street noises filled my ears. Even the occasional ship horn blasted. Overwhelmed by the noise and chaos I could not help thinking how different it was from the simple, quiet place I had left not many days before.

With lighted buildings, neon lights, cars, street vendors cooking hot dogs, and people going here and there it was impossible to see and hear everything that was going on. I wondered where all those people were going, yet they all seemed to know and were also in a big hurry to get there. They surely were not reading the lighted messages either. Times Square was just a big sea of movement—moving cars, moving people, moving lights.

I could not help but notice the military recruiting office as it sat prominently in Times Square. I made a mental note of where we turned to go to our hotel so I would know exactly how to get there by foot the next day.

Turning off Times Square a short distance, we arrived at our hotel. With my leather suitcase in one hand, guitar in the other and the remaining $10 in my pocket, I made my way to my room. The room was adequate and clean with a bed, desk and chair, and a radio. A window looked onto a backyard. After all the hustle and bustle of Times Square, the room was surprisingly quiet. A newspaper, perhaps a New York Times, was on the desk. I remember that I attempted to read it, but with my limited English I couldn't understand what I was reading.

Up to the age of six, English had been my first and native language, but for the next fourteen years I was totally immersed in German and had forgotten most of the English I knew. We did study English in school, but it was Shakespearean English and I did not find that people in New York were speaking or writing in Shakespearean style.

The radio in the room really intrigued me. I was interested to see how the radio programs here compared to those I had listened to in Germany. I turned the radio on and began dialing stations, hoping to learn something of this very exciting and captivating place. Even with my limited English I could tell that the programs were often interrupted by commercials and that every hour on the hour they reported five minutes of news.

German radio was quite different. The government controlled everything, including the radio. For instance, they never allowed programs to be interrupted by commercials. Commercials had specified times, but I did not know anyone who really listened to them.

During the Nazi regime the only legal source of information was the government radio broadcasts. Shortwave radios were forbidden because those who owned them could get information from America and all over the world. No one dared get caught with that type of radio. As I understood it, anyone caught listening to unauthorized broadcasts was sent away to reeducation camps. After the war, radio was still controlled by the government which funded the programs by collecting a monthly fee, taxation by another name. Unfortunately, *we* paid for what *they* wanted to give us. Just as before, government agents still monitored radios that were active. If they found anyone listening who had not subscribed, that person would be fined.

When I was a teenager, I did not have the subscription money and was also concerned that they might still be monitoring what we were listening to. However, occasionally I wanted to listen to popular music, especially from America. In order to at least avoid the fee, I kept my radio in "repair status." When I wanted to listen to it, I knew how to get it working again. When I was finished listening, I put it back in repair status.

On this apparently free radio in my New York City hotel room, I hoped to find some American music like Elvis. His music was, of course, never played on the government-controlled radio stations in Germany, but I had enjoyed hearing him on the Armed Forces Radio. However, I didn't find anything familiar to me or that I was interested in listening to.

I was very tired from this exhilarating and stimulating day so I turned off the radio and went to bed. My first night's sleep back in America!

CHAPTER 2

Times Square Recruitment

Waking up on my first morning back in the US, I was confident I would be OK but I had no idea what would become of me in this great country. The possibilities seemed endless and incomprehensible. Unlike some of the immigrants on the ship, I did not have a job offer awaiting me.

The American Consulate in Stuttgart had impressed upon me that when I arrived in America, I needed to get in touch with a recruiter immediately because the US still had the draft. Due to my experience in Germany, I would never have considered doing anything other than what I was instructed by the Consulate. In Germany we were taught to obey authority. But more importantly, I had a relationship with the Consulate. I had remained in contact with them and they kept up with me and were interested in my well-being. I trusted them and what they told me to do. I felt like they were sort of my guardian and my connection to America.

I dressed and again with my suitcase in one hand and guitar in the other I headed out for the most famous military recruiting office in the US—Times Square!

I was a little hungry and despite the cold I stopped on the way and bought a hot dog from a street vendor. I was accustomed to street vendors in Germany so this felt familiar and comforting to me.

I wondered what exactly would happen at the recruiting office. I was accustomed to the requirement in Germany that we keep the local authorities abreast of any change of address. Perhaps this visit to the recruiting office was just to notify them that I, an American citizen, was now in New York. Or perhaps I would be drafted right away.

Since I had no money or job and always wanted to fly I hoped the Air Force needed me right away. But would I qualify for the Air Force and flight school or would they put me in another branch? Would I have to find a job until they needed me in the military? Would it be possible to fulfill my dream of going to Florida, which was warm and seemed particularly appealing right now?

That morning I walked into the recruiting office and out of the cold, cold weather. In stark contrast to the hustle and bustle of Times Square I was the only client for the four recruiters; the situation remained the same through the whole process. The room was long and narrow with four desks lined up perpendicular to the wall, a desk for each branch of the military. A recruiter, wearing his sharp dress uniform, represented each branch. Naturally, the Marine desk was the first one.

I asked to talk to the Air Force recruiter who was at the last desk in the back of the room. The Marine pointed me to the Army desk and told me that only the Army was taking recruits right now. Somehow he made it perfectly clear.

I went to the Army recruiter, sat down and gave him the paperwork I had brought from the Consulate. As he read through the documents, he seemed pleased that he had a really good deal for me! He tried to explain that they would train me on what sounded like the latest and greatest that the Army had. He would sign me up for only two years. I could join the Army and they would send me back to Germany!

The last thing I wanted to do was go back to Germany and I did not want to be in the Army. I dug ditches, hauled bricks for masons, and even borrowed some of the money in order to come back to the US. I wanted to stay here! I really wanted to fly and I wanted to go to the sunshine and warm beaches of Florida. But in Germany I had learned that what you want and what you get are not always the same; I assumed the military was no different.

The recruiter explained that I needed to go to Whitehall Street to be officially processed into the Army. The fact that there was another step in the process gave me hope that the Air Force might still be an option. But with the situation being as it was—very cold outside, me with no money and no job—I reluctantly signed on the dotted line, still hoping that something would be different at Whitehall Street. The recruiter gave me enough tokens for the subway and the ferry to Fort Jay on Governors Island for an overnight stay, and for the trip back to Whitehall the following day. Getting to Governors Island via the subway and ferry proved to be quite easy for me.

At Fort Jay, I was assigned to a room that had four beds. With only one other man there, I pretty much had my choice of the other beds, not that one was any more appealing than the other. I tried to talk to the other man a bit, but he was kind of quiet. I hoped to get some kind of information from him about the military or even life in America but all I learned was that he was a GI and I didn't find out which branch. The mess hall at Fort Jay served cafeteria-style military food. None of this cost me any money and for that I was grateful.

CHAPTER 3

Whitehall Street Induction Center

The next morning I set out, again with my suitcase and guitar, for Whitehall. I retraced my route on the ferry and back to the subway. I entered the subway station, set my belongings down and walked over to check the track plan and schedule. The recruiter told me which track I needed to be on to get to Whitehall but a bit of important information was missing. I realized I needed to refer to the track plan to determine which side of the track I should be on to catch the train in the right direction.

A gentleman standing near my suitcase called to me and told me that I should not leave my belongings unattended. His warning was the first clue I had that I needed to be aware of my surroundings. After all, New York was a big city and I guess people might take something left, even momentarily, unattended. How could I possibly have been this naïve after my experiences in Germany! I guess I thought I was in America now and I was safe.

I went to the appropriate side of the track and when the subway came, I got on. I had no idea how far it was to my stop. So once on the train, I started asking people where I would have to get off to go to Whitehall Street. It surprised me that no one knew; they just seemed to know where to get on and off for their daily commute. After a while I began to get nervous that I might miss my stop, so I decided I would get off, go up to street level, and perhaps I would be able to figure it out from there. When I got onto the street, a street sign right in front of me said, "Whitehall." What a relief! I had the building number so after a short walk, I was there.

Whitehall was a big building and to my amazement, the place was absolutely packed with people. Here, lines and lines of recruits waited to be processed in. Still hoping to join the Air Force, I slowly worked my way through the dense crowd asking people which recruiter they were waiting to see. Eventually, I found those waiting for the Air Force and I got in that line.

Everything was very efficient but nevertheless very slow. I had time to look around and wonder where all these people had come from—certainly not the lonely recruiting office at Times Square! Since the Army was supposedly the only branch recruiting, I was curious about why so many people stood in queues for the other branches.

Eventually I reached the front of the line and handed the guy behind the desk my papers from Times Square. He looked at the papers and said, "You are in the wrong line, the Army is over there!" I responded that I did not want to be in the Army, I wanted to be in the Air Force. He kept looking at me and I stood right there just looking back at him. I was *not* going to move.

I really wanted to be in the Air Force. And in that moment as I stood there staring at him and he stared back at me, I reflected on having always been interested in airplanes. Even back when I was in first grade in the Goudy School in Chicago, I had drawn a picture of an airplane which was printed right by my name in the yearbook. I have that yearbook to this day. In Germany I had annoyed my friends on more than one occasion when we were playing soccer and an airplane flew overhead. For me the soccer game was no longer the focus as I stopped and watched the plane go by.

Eventually, our staring contest came to an end. I guess he wanted to move things along, so he reached under his desk, pulled out a paper and said, "Sign this!" He copied all my information from the Army papers, tore them up and threw them in the trash can. He, un-

Picture Wes drew of an airplane that was printed in his yearbook at the Goudy School, 1942–43

like the Army recruiter, did not tell me where I would be going, what I would be doing or even if I was now being inducted into the Air Force. Perhaps I was just being registered or possibly checked to determine if I was qualified for service. He explained nothing and made no promises at all–just got my signature on the paper. Little did I know at that time that I had just signed up for four years in the Air Force rather than the two years in the Army. It was February 5, 1958!

Now the processing really began and again it was very efficient, but involved standing in this line and that line, more paperwork, some tests and information about my background. I suppose they were trying to determine my aptitude for various jobs in the Air Force. The questions were difficult for me and I did not do particularly well. A typical American recruit probably knew a lot of the terms, but they were foreign to me. For example, I was asked something about the use of a Mae West. Although I had actually used a Mae West in Germany, I certainly did not know it by that name. Shakespeare did not prepare me for this!

I don't remember if there were any vaccinations involved, but I am pretty sure there were. For me, the most memorable and awkward part of this entire day was all of us standing in the naked line-up, shoulder-to-shoulder! We all had to strip and stand in line until a doctor came and checked each of us, front and back.

This was the beginning of my new life in America. I was finally back where I belonged.

This is to Certify that *Adolf Juergen Kesselhorst* was born in the Norwegian-American Hospital Date *Tuesday Sept 8 1936@ 12:53 AM CST* Weight *8* Lbs. *3* Ounces

This Certificate being duly signed by the Attending Physician, Superintendent and the Corporate Seal affixed hereon.

Birth Certificate,
Chicago, 1936

CHAPTER 4

Childhood in Chicago

Chicago, September 1936. I was born an American citizen in Chicago, Illinois, on September 8, 1936. My parents had emigrated from Germany to the United States in the 1920s. They met, fell in love, and married in Chicago. Although they were not yet citizens, they had been here long enough that they were very Americanized. They dressed like Americans, listened to American music, went to American movies, and did the American dances of the time. English was our household language. They never spoke German to me or around me.

Although it was the Depression years, we managed to live a fairly normal middle-class, big-city lifestyle. We did not own a car, but everything was accessible either by walking or public transportation. My parents managed the apartment building in which we lived on Kenmore Avenue. The apartment was small but plenty adequate for the three of us. In the living room was a Murphy bed; an enclosed porch held another bed. My dad often slept on the porch because he enjoyed opening the windows and having the fresh air. Their work at the apartment building allowed us to be together as a family a great deal of the time.

As I got a little older and when the weather was warm, we took a lot of family outings to the zoo, the park or to the beach which was not many blocks away. We have pictures of us playing on the beach with the Edgewater Hotel in the background. My dad bought me a toy sailboat that we took to Lake Michigan to sail along the shoreline on the beach. Like a lot of little boys, I enjoyed wearing my sailor suit.

My babysitter was really not much older than I was and kind of like a member of the family. She came along on a lot of our family outings. I had a tricycle and later a bicycle. She and I used to ride our bikes

In Chicago. Above, Wes in sailor suit at the park
Opposite page, Wes on the beach and on his tricycle

About 1938, Wes and his mother in Chicago

About 1938, Wes and his father in Chicago

together. As it turns out, bicycling would continue to be a big part of my life.

My mother was quite in tune with American fashion and was always very well-dressed. My dad liked to tell me what a good dancer she was. Before she married my dad, she worked in the textile industry. She liked to embroider linens for our home and for gifts. She especially enjoyed American songs and kept a notebook in which she would write the lyrics to her favorites. I liked it when she would sing the songs. She kept a map of the US on the wall, and as a preschooler I had learned all the states in the union, all forty-eight of them.

My dad was a quiet man. He, like my mother, was always dressed nicely, much like the men during that time. He usually wore a suit and hat. He was a good family man and seemed to really enjoy our family outings.

At Christmas time, my family would dress warmly and as was customary then, we strolled along downtown Chicago streets looking at the beautiful festive displays. I think Neiman Marcus had an elaborate miniature window display. The holiday scene was completely animated and so life-like that to me it was real and alive. It was absolutely magical!

I made friends with several boys about my age in the neighborhood; we played hide-and-seek and rode bikes together. Another boy my age lived upstairs in our apartment building. I remember one Halloween I went with him and his dad to a spook house someplace. I find it funny how little things like that stick in my memory while some of the real significant ones have a way of escaping.

In one of the apartments lived a cowboy-type young man whose hobby was leatherwork. He made me a beautiful western-style, tooled leather belt. It had a metal tip on the end and a beautiful buckle. I had that belt for a very long time. Whenever I visited him, he enjoyed making me a waffle on his waffle iron. Being a growing little boy, I would not turn down a delicious waffle.

I always liked to tinker with things. When people moved out of the apartments, they often would leave behind their clocks and radios. I have no idea why they left those particular things but I liked to take the clocks apart and put them back together. These were, of course, the old style wind-up alarm clocks. Little did I know that not too long after this, I would be taking apart far less innocent things.

A drug store on a nearby corner had a soda fountain. I liked to go there and sometimes people would just be nice to me and buy me some ice cream or soda. People were friendly and kind in those days in our Chicago neighborhood.

When I was four years old, I suddenly became very ill. My dad rushed me to the hospital but my appendix had already ruptured. This was pretty much a death sentence in 1940, so the doctors just put clamps in the incision and put me off in a room by myself, apparently to die. But it was not to be, since the next morning I was still alive, they decided I might actually live and they began to nurse me back to health. The clamps left a pretty ugly scar but at least I survived. That was my first brush with death.

I was only four when this happened but somehow I had a feeling that a greater power was involved. My parents were not churchgoers but over the years they instilled in me their own belief that there is a God. Their belief was evidenced to me by their awe of nature, animals, and creation in general. I believed that God had surely been with me through my ordeal.

In Chicago I started school when I was six, like most children. However, my first time to attend first grade would not be my last. The Goudy School was within walking distance from our home. Every morning, the first thing we did was stand, place our hand over our heart and say the Pledge of Allegiance. Although this was 1942, nine months after Pearl Harbor, I was not aware of the Japanese attack or that we were at war with Japan or Germany. My parents never discussed anything political with me. All in all, my life was just happy and carefree.

Then suddenly, my dad was gone for a while. I was not sure how long or why he was away. For all I knew it was work-related. The first time I really knew that things were not OK was when several men showed up and ransacked our apartment. My mother and I were alone of course. They asked all kinds of questions and apparently were looking for something. They pulled out the drawers and dumped the contents on the floor. They also went through all the closets. They must not have found anything because they left without taking anything with them.

I could not then, and still cannot, imagine what they might have thought could be in our apartment that would be of any concern to anyone. I was six years old and very frightened by this experience. My mother was very composed, but I knew she too was frightened.

When my dad came back home, he brought shipping trunks with him. I think he had three of them. They had a place to hang clothes and also had drawers. My parents packed these trunks with the items they especially wanted to keep, mainly clothes. My dad left again for some time and while he was away, the trunks just sat in our apartment. My mother and I stayed there alone.

Aerial views of Crystal City Family Internment Camp
General Photograph Collection, UTSA Special Collections

CHAPTER 5

Internment in Crystal City, Texas

Crystal City, Texas, Spring 1943. I was still six years old, in the spring of 1943, when my mother and I were reunited with my father. My parents and I were taken by train under armed guard to Crystal City, Texas. During daylight hours on the train my parents kept me entertained by pointing out sights along the way. At night we slept in sleeper cars. I really had no idea what was going on. I did not know that the country was at war. My parents just did not discuss such matters with me or around me.

On March 25, 1943, we arrived at the train platform at Crystal City. A lot of armed guards waited for us. They put everyone from the train on the back of flatbed trucks and took us to the Crystal City Family Internment Camp. We passed through a gate into the camp and I could see the high barbed wire fence and armed guard towers. The truck stopped and we were taken off, all still under armed guards. The men were told to go and find a place for their families. Even though he didn't know anyone in the camp, my dad stopped at one of the huts nearby and asked if my mother and I could wait with the family while he looked for a place for us to stay. They were willing so we waited there.

While we were there, the family gave their cat a bath in the sink. Naturally, the cat was not very agreeable. For me this was quite a show since I had never had a pet of any kind. An hour or two later, my dad returned. He had found a hut for us to live in while we were there.

I later learned that Crystal City is located about a hundred miles south of San Antonio, not far from the Mexican border, in a sparsely populated area. Before it was used as a family internment camp, Crystal City was just a small farming community and the self-proclaimed Spinach Capital of the World. Their town landmark is a big statue of Popeye!

At the time I had no idea where we were, but this was a colossal change of environment for me. Chicago was, of course, a large, thriving city, but here we were in an isolated, desert-like, no-man's land. Here, hardly any vehicles ever drove on the streets but snakes, scorpions, centipedes, spiders, horny toads, and roadrunners were everywhere. From time to time everything had to be removed from the house and the fire department came in to hose the inside of the hut to get rid of the critters. No trees grew except for a small orange orchard. Castor bean plants were common in the camp, but they were more like shrubs than trees. The weather was mostly hot and dry. Tumbleweeds blew around. Also, unlike Chicago it was very quiet. The only sounds I remember hearing were the saws in the nearby woodshop. A natural waterhole in the camp was used for irrigation. On more than one occasion the guards had to "dispatch" a puma that had jumped the barbed wire fence. I was amazed that they could jump that high and that they were even there.

The most striking difference from Chicago was that we were now held behind a ten-foot barbed wire fence with several armed guard towers along it and Rangers who rode their horses around the outside perimeter of the fence. We were not free to leave. We were internees.

As I remember it, our hut was a single-family unit with one room about twelve by eighteen feet. I think the room had three windows and one door leading to the outside. The room held an icebox, two beds, a small table and some chairs, and a small heater. We had no running water, and of course, no sewer drainage, toilet or shower. We did not have a stove on which to cook. Community showers and toilet facilities were available in separate buildings within walking distance. A dining facility served food nearby but

The quiet emptiness of Crystal City, in such contrast to life in Chicago, German child looking toward the German School
General Photograph Collection, UTSA Special Collections

I do not remember it or even eating there. Every day ice and milk were delivered to each of the huts.

The camp population consisted of German Americans, Japanese Americans and as I later learned, Latin Americans of German and Japanese ancestry. Each had its own section of the camp. I also later learned that many of the internees were American citizens like me. They were American spouses or American-born children of immigrants who had been "detained."

Three schools served the camp: a German, a Japanese and an American school. I attended the German one. At that school and to some extent in the camp, I was exposed for the first time to a bit of German culture. My parents and I had lived as Americans and had not observed German customs.

I didn't know any German words or even a single German song. Since all the instruction was in German, I had to start over in first grade for the second, but still not my last, time. When I had homework, I did it at a small table in our hut.

Around the camp, when I was not in school, my clothing was very simple. I wore only a pair of shorts, no shirt or shoes. I spent my days in the camp exploring. I liked to pick up little snakes, put them in my pocket and take them home. My mother didn't like that too much.

I also liked to collect rocks. Some were really colorful and I could not figure out where they had come from. This desert area didn't have a river or mountains or any source for these pretty stones. My solution was they had fallen from the sky. I was searching for meteor rocks and I was quite sure I had found

Guard tower and high fence, patrolled by Texas Rangers, Crystal City Internment Camp   Virginia W Davis Archives of Southwest Texas

some! I kept those rocks with me and may even have them to this day.

I made some friends who lived near me that were about my age. We liked to play Cowboys and Indians. Someone in the woodshop made us wooden guns to play with.

Some older boys who lived nearby liked to buy airplane kits in the craft store. Being fascinated by airplanes, I found their projects quite interesting. The planes operated by wind-up rubber bands. I liked watching the boys out on the street in front of our house. They would wind up the rubber bands and launch the airplanes into the air. They never flew very far but that didn't matter to me—I just liked seeing them fly.

From that same craft store I enjoyed buying and reading comic books that were very futuristic. I read Dick Tracy, Superman and other high-tech comics. In my child-like understanding, the only way these otherwise normal human beings could do such extraordinary things surely was through a higher power. I also bought several Wild West picture postcards, which I managed to hang on to somehow and still have in a scrapbook.

Everyone, it seemed, attempted to make a normal life in these very abnormal circumstances. They put a lot of effort into making the place less bleak and more productive. My mother had morning glories that bloomed by the door and my dad grew cantaloupe out front. Other internees planted flowers and vegetable gardens as well. The German Americans built a beer garden. I have a picture of my dad and other German American men sitting around a long table enjoying their beer and camaraderie.

Wild West picture postcard from shop in Crystal City

The German beer garden in Crystal City

The German Americans and Japanese Americans were kept in separate parts of the camp. However, my dad became friends with one Japanese American who gave him a New Year's card that he had hand-painted. I still have that card in my scrapbook. Through their friendship we were invited to a play the Japanese were putting on. The costumes, makeup, music, and gestures were very different from anything I had been exposed to before. I couldn't understand what was going on or its meaning, but I found it fascinating. Little did I know that one day I would be living in Japan.

Other activities helped us create a sense of normalcy. My dad was a firefighter in the volunteer fire department. A lot of people used the woodcraft shop to make wood carvings and toys. These crafts were then displayed for a kind of show-and-tell for everyone to enjoy. One of the German Americans was a scientist of some sort. He collected various types of bugs, caterpillars, butterflies, and other critters and had them pinned up on boards with all of them identified by their scientific and common names, a display like one might expect to see in a museum or a college. I liked to go there and see his collection which I found to be interesting. I was amazed that out there in that desert area he was able to find all those things.

I do not remember Christmas that year. We did however get a booklet of Christmas hymns including "Silent Night." All the songs were in German. It was "a gift from the Mennonite Central Committee in Akron, Pennsylvania, who arranged for its publication and distribution through the War Prisoners' Aid of the Y.M.C.A." Like all printed material that came into the camp, it had been censored. The US Office of Censorship stamp on the front stated that it was "examined by 539." I still have that booklet.

A hospital served the camp and I suppose the care was sufficient. We did have to use it on a couple of

From booklet of German Christmas hymns, Crystal City provided by Mennonite Central Committee

Maypole dance, Crystal City

occasions. My dad had a situation that he thought could be taken care of just by eating castor beans off the trees. Everyone was familiar with castor oil and its uses in those days. What he didn't know was that the natural castor bean has a very poisonous oil that has to be processed out before the castor oil can be safely consumed. He became very ill and was in the hospital quite a while getting over that.

In my case I was running around with my friends having an intense game of cowboys and Indians. Probably everyone, like me, was barefoot. We were playing on a loading ramp and I jumped off onto a board that had a rusty nail sticking up which went right through my bare foot. At the camp hospital they cleaned my foot up and probably gave me a shot.

In May, the German Americans celebrated the traditional Maypole dance for teenagers. I cannot imagine how or from where they managed to get such a big tree to use for this purpose. It was perfectly straight, about twenty or thirty feet high. The tree was stripped of its bark then set upright in the ground. A wreath hung down from the top loaded with presents. The boys tried to climb the slippery pole to get to the gifts. Some of the boys were successful; I am not sure how many. Then the boys and girls danced around the pole.

Traditionally long ribbons of different colors hung from the top of the tree. Each dancer held onto a ribbon and danced around the Maypole in such a way that the ribbon wove a pattern down the shaft. They then reversed the dance so that the ribbons were unwound. Everyone had to know his or her part and do it correctly. At Crystal City we did not have the ribbons but the young people still danced around the pole as if they did.

I had never seen a Maypole dance before and I was too young to participate, but I found the German music and dancing fun to hear and observe. Everyone seemed to be having a good time. I guess we had a temporary reprieve from the awareness that we were being held behind a barbed wire fence.

While I was at Crystal City, the irrigation pond was drained to create a swimming pool. As the men drained out the water, they collected the snakes that were in it. They collected two 55-gallon barrels half-full with snakes. I was glad I had never been tempted to go swimming in the pond! I was still there when the concrete was poured and was curing. The older kids used the dry pool as a roller skating rink. With South Texas being so hot and dry, I am sure that the internees welcomed the pool once it was filled with water.

CHAPTER 6

The Swedish Exchange Ship
Gripsholm

SS Gripsholm, **February 1944.** In the wee hours of
the night on February 12, 1944, my parents and I were
taken under armed guard from Crystal City Family
Internment Camp. We boarded a train with many
other German American families from the camp.
Of course, I did not know our destination. I was now
seven years old.

Always under armed guard, we traveled a long distance to a New Jersey shipyard. Here we were queued
to board the *SS Gripsholm*. Again I had no idea where
we were or where we were going. From the pier as we
waited to board the ship, I watched the longshoremen
load everyone's belongings onto the ship. Cranes
lifted large nets filled with people's household goods
and swung them over the cargo hold. But instead of
lowering them down, they opened the nets and let
everything free-fall into the hold. I was concerned
about what was happening to our possessions.

Unlike the other transfers that had been conducted
at night, we boarded the ship in daylight. My family
located our room and settled in. The ship sailed on

February 15, 1944 into the rough North Atlantic seas. This time of year, in this part of the ocean, very rough seas are quite normal. I was seasick for several days of the trip, so I stayed in our room a lot and watched out the porthole and at times watched the destroyers that were escorting our ship across the Atlantic. At night our ship was lit up with bright lights. I did not know why at the time, but later it was clear to me. The lights, for one, signaled that this was a diplomatic, neutral ship that was guaranteed safe passage by all belligerents. In addition, the lights acted much like a bug spray repelling the other ships. They did not want to be near us because the light would silhouette them on the dark sea, giving away their position. Even with the "safe passage" agreement and all the lights, the voyage was very dangerous because the waters were infested with German U-boats.

On February 25, 1944, we arrived in Lisbon, Portugal. We stayed in Lisbon a couple of days in a nice hotel. We were given the time to shop for clothes warm enough for Europe's winter season and we bought some very nice winter clothing there.

From Lisbon we went by train into Germany. I am not sure the exact route, but we entered Germany at Saarbrucken. From there we went to Hamburg, where my father's family lived in Steinkirchen by the Elbe River.

For whatever reason, my parents did not talk to me about the war or what was being done with us. Maybe they hoped to protect me; I was so very young. I think my awareness that we were at war and that we were involved in some way gradually evolved as I watched things happen to us and around us—my dad being gone, the men coming in and searching our apartment, going on the train and being behind barbed wire at Crystal City, going on the train to the docks, watching the longshoremen handling our baggage, looking out the porthole and watching the destroyers that were escorting us, entering Germany at Saarbrucken and then—the bombings in Hamburg....

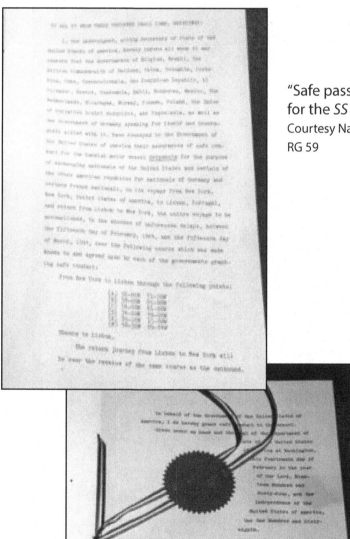

"Safe passage guarantee" for the *SS Gripsholm*
Courtesy National Archives, RG 59

Both pages. The *Gripsholm* in port, and loading passengers' belongings. Courtesy National Archives, Box RG 59

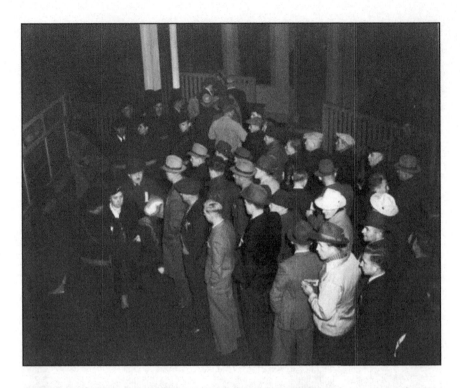

Both pages. Residents from internment camps boarding the *Gripsholm.* Courtesy National Archives, Box RG 59

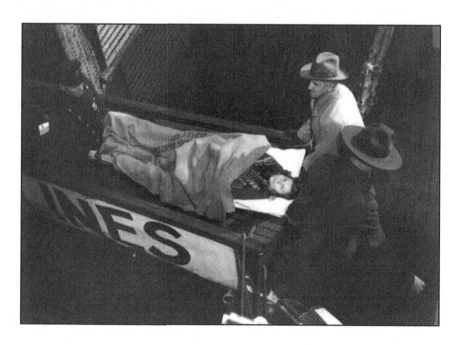

Map showing bombing approaches to Hamburg. Steinkirchen was inside the inner circle. The numbers show how many minutes it took for different types of bombers to reach and bomb Hamburg. This let people know how much time they had to get to a bunker or another safer location.

CHAPTER 7

Hamburg, Germany

Hamburg / Steinkirchen, Germany, February 1944.
While I did not know these things about Hamburg at
the age of seven, I find it important to explain here.

During World War II, Hamburg was a strategic
target for the Allies. Not only was it a huge port on
the North Sea, but the city had oil refineries, ship-
yards, U-boat yards and a great deal of industry. The
Elbe River, very deep and wide, was a major waterway
across Europe. The Elbe was also Germany's access to
the North Sea and thus the Atlantic Ocean. The Allies
had already bombed Hamburg quite extensively
before we went to Germany. But the bombing raids
continued until the war ended.

Steinkirchen (Fliegeraufnahme)

Village of Steinkirchen, Germany

CHAPTER 8

Steinkirchen

Hamburg/Steinkirchen, Germany, February 1944. I do not remember exactly how we got there, but I do remember some sort of processing when our train reached Saarbrucken. Once we were cleared, the people around me grew noticeably quieter and a hush spread. I am not sure what they might have seen or were thinking. I was just seven years old and really did not understand anything that was going on. But eventually we got to Steinkirchen and to my grandparents' home.

In the spring of 1944, Hamburg and the surrounding area was still under attack by the Allies. Life was very hard for the people living there but they had to go on somehow in spite of the raids. Steinkirchen is a suburb of Hamburg, just across the Elbe River on the western side, right along the approach path of the allied bombers.

The area around Steinkirchen was very beautiful in the spring. Miles and miles of cherry trees bloomed along the levees. I remember how picturesque they were and that the smell was splendid. Naturally many bees swarmed around.

After the long, cold winters, coming to see the cherry trees was an annual event for the city's people. Even during the war years some tourists still ventured out during bombing lulls to come and enjoy the beautiful blossoms and fragrant smells. Despite fewer visitors, air raids and fires, God's universe carried on with its ever-changing seasons. Winter turned to Spring and the oblivious cherry trees faithfully produced their flowers and the diligent bees worked on, no matter what.

These cherries trees were not only scenic. They were also an important food crop for the people in the area. I learned there were several varieties which bloomed in succession, providing a long season of beauty and fruit. My favorite was the Bing cherry with its robust flavor.

Steinkirchen is quite far north, on a latitude that crosses Canada about 150 miles south of Ketchikan, Alaska. But due to the Gulf Stream, it was not as cold as might be expected. However, much like Alaska, the winter months were mostly dark with very few day-light hours. Besides the darkness, a lot of fog, rain and snow meant that it was essential to own a slicker and a Sou'wester rain hat. How different all that was from the dry, sunbaked, virtually treeless southern Texas I had just left.

In the summer occasionally severe thunderstorms swept over the area. The land was flat and the build-up of clouds took over the whole scene, billowing up and up into the sky in spectacular cloud formations. I had never seen mountains and I imagined that these thunderstorms must be what mountains looked like.

Apparently the Allies had developed somewhat accurate weather forecasting because the prediction of thunderstorms brought us welcomed relief from bombing raids. During this lull, we would take a chance on the weather and go to play in the water on the Elbe River, which had a nice beach. On one such occasion we were not so lucky and the weather caught us on the way home. Though we did not have to be concerned about bombings, the lightning all around scared us enough.

The home of Wes' grandparents in Steinkirchen

CHAPTER 9

My Grandparents' Home

While my grandparents did graciously take us in, I am sure it was difficult to have a family move in with them during their retirement years, much less during a war. The house was not very large, certainly not a two-family home. My grandmother had died when my father was very young. My grandfather remarried some years later so his wife was actually my step-grandmother. She had never met any of us before.

My great-grandfather and his family had originally owned the property, a fairly large plot of land along the Luhe River, a tributary to the Elbe River which was less than a mile away. He had a large *fachwerk* (half-timbered) house with a thatched roof and a hard-packed dirt floor. They rented out the front of the house to two other families.

My great-grandfather had been a block-and-tackle maker for sailing ships of that time. He made them of wood in his shop, which was a large room inside his home. This house was still standing and so I went there from time to time and looked through his workshop hoping to find some of his tools. Many of them had already been removed, but I managed to find a few hand tools which I still have.

My grandparents had built a smaller brick home on the property for their retirement home. The main entrance to the house was in the middle and opened into a hallway. Just inside a stairway led to the small upstairs bedrooms. To the right was a large living room called *Die Gute Stube*. In America we would call it a formal living room. It had nice furniture and was used for entertaining. This room took up the entire right side of the house.

The room on the left served as sort of a combined family room and dining area. The family used this room daily to sit, read and have our meals. It held a sofa, a coal burning stove, a bookcase hanging on the wall, the dining table and a radio. My dad, who was often away working in Hamburg, slept on the sofa in this room when he was there. The kitchen, a pantry and a door leading to the basement were on the back side of this family room. Our family normally stored potatoes, apples and other fruit in the basement during the winter.

I shared a bedroom with my mother upstairs on the left. The area to the right was divided into two rooms. The back part was my grandparents' bedroom and the tiny front room was empty for a while. These rooms were all quite small and the slanted attic ceilings reduced the usable space considerably.

In the backyard stood a three-room brick building. One was a washroom with a cistern that collected rainwater from the roof of the house. The cistern had a hand pump on it and we used this unheated water for bathing. A big metal pot sat over a brick fire pit where my grandparents heated water for laundry. We stored firewood and coal in the middle room. The third room was the outhouse. Naturally it was always cold. It had a seat that looked like a toilet, but of course, it could not be flushed. Gravity pulled the waste down into a holding tank below. My grandfather removed the contents through an outside access and used it as fertilizer for the fruit trees on the property.

We had a chicken coop out back with hens and a rooster so we always had chickens and eggs. When a hen got old and quit laying, she became dinner—too tough for anything but a soup or stew. There was also a pigsty but no pigs when I was there.

Our property ran right up to the levee on the Luhe River, a tributary to the Elbe River. We were responsible for inspecting and reporting the condition of the levee. At times when there was a high tide, the water came almost to the top of the levee which required a full inspection after the water receded. With a war going on, we had much more to be troubled about concerning the levee.

The home and surroundings in Steinkirchen were designed to function very well during peacetime. But, of course, everything was different for everyone when we went there in 1944. We had to live off the land as best we could. For me, life seemed to continually change; I simply had to adjust to that.

Some changes were positive. I'd never had a pet before and our family cat, Budabu, was a real comfort to me. He also kept rats and mice under control.

Among the many things I had to adjust to was the shortage of food, as well as my grandfather's very simple but strict dining rules. The ladies brought food from the kitchen and put it on the dining table. When my grandfather started eating everybody started eating; when he finished everybody was finished. The ladies might have had their own rules when they got back to the kitchen. I was seven years old and not old enough to sit at the table, I had to eat standing. I was also not allowed to converse. My dad was able to get the rules altered a bit so that at least I could sit at the table but still could not speak.

The meal always began with a bowl of soup; its purpose was to give us more of a feeling of being full because we didn't have a lot to eat. If there was any dessert at all, it would be made from the cherries or other fruit on the property. We, of course, did not have ice cream, which I had enjoyed so much in America. If we needed a snack we would go to the basement for fruit. We had to pick the ones that showed signs of going bad because if we picked a good one all the ones left would eventually be nothing but rotten fruit.

The starlings came in huge swarms when the trees had fruit. The birds had a real heyday with all that fruit. They would peck a piece of fruit, never eating the whole thing but ruining it just the same. My grandfather used his shotgun to keep them under control and provide for our supper. It took quite a few starlings, about six per person, to feed all of us. Fortunately my grandfather was a good shot. Since the imprudent birds lined up right along a branch he could often kill six or more with one shot.

My grandfather was also good at fishing for eel. He knew that a sheep floating in the river marked a good time and place to catch eels. He had a special type of lure that he made from things around the house. He put a cone-shaped paper in the sand and put a stiff wire down through the center. He then heated lead and poured it into the paper. When it cooled, he had a piece of cone-shaped, hard lead with a wire through the center sticking out both ends. He then bent the wire on the bottom into a coil. On the top he put a loop in the wire and tied it to a fishing pole.

He had a way of stringing up lots of nightcrawlers which he then tied onto the bottom wire. He dropped this into the river and situated it so the lure was barely above the bottom. The eels would come and start to eat the nightcrawlers but could not pull them off the string. When he felt the eels, he would pull the lure up and hold the lure over the boat; the eels would then fall off. He did this over and over until he had enough eels for dinner.

Now, skinning the eels was a job! First he put sand on his hands so that he could grip the slippery eel behind the head, then chop the head almost off. The eel had several skins and holding the head he pulled them off one by one. From the skinned eel the women made eel soup, a specialty around Hamburg. It has a distinct taste and my grandmother made it excellently.

We had three drainage ditches, one in front of the house parallel with the road and one on each side of the house. This was low-lying land and the ditches were necessary to channel the water away. I was amused by the life in the very clear water of the ditches. Stichlinge, which were little fish about a finger long, thrived in the ditches. They were called *stichlinge* because they had needle-like things sticking out, one on the top and one out of each side for natural protection. They were beautiful with all sorts of colors and were just fascinating to watch. Also frogs, leeches, and rats lived in the water. For me nature had provided a self-maintaining aquarium right there on the property.

I still liked to scavenge around on the ground and actually found, and still have, a petrified sea urchin. Many, many years ago our property had been ocean bottom and I guessed that the sea urchin was from that time. As changes in the earth took place, the Elbe and Luhe Rivers were formed.

We, of course, did not have the luxury of a swimming pool. There were no formal swimming lessons like many American children have today. In Steinkirchen children learned to swim in the Luhe River which was not clear; it was silt. A parent or older child tied a rope around the child's chest and threw them into the river. They used the rope to hold the child securely as they thrashed about and eventually learned to swim.

I did not find this method of learning to swim at all appealing. Somehow I got a Mae West, an aviator's life vest that once inflated gave the wearer the appearance of having very large breasts, much like its namesake. At the time I did not know it was called that. I put it on, blew it up by mouth and got in the river. As I became better at swimming—if you can call what I did swimming—I gradually put less and less air in the Mae West until I did not need it at all.

My dad was able to get a bicycle for transportation and cleverly had it converted to a woman's bike since all the men's bikes were confiscated for the war effort. He used the bike to haul items that we were not able to carry by hand. I was amazed at the loads he could carry on that bike. He would go to other farms in the area and barter for things we needed and he would come peddling back loaded down with goods. Often he would bring a big sack of potatoes. Our property would not grow potatoes, but nearby farms having sandy soil grew potatoes very well.

The village had Russian prisoners of war, some of whom were released during the day to provide labor for people in the local community. One of them worked for our family. He was a cobbler. He made my grandfather a nice pair of work boots. New shoes or boots were simply not available during the war so this soldier did my grandfather a great service. They assigned me the job of cleaning the boots and shoes. We, of course, had no polish. Another job they gave me was darning socks, but I guess I wasn't too good at that because I didn't have that job long. I also had to help cut the roots for firewood.

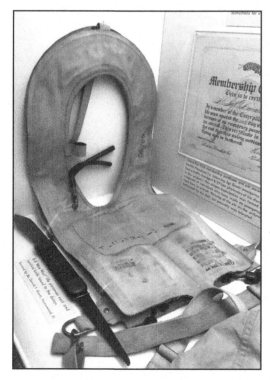

"Mae West" similar to the one Wes wore to learn to swim, a bright yellow aviator's water survival vest
Photo of exhibit at National Museum of the US Air Force, Dayton, Ohio

CHAPTER 10

First Grade Again

In Germany I had to go to first grade yet another time. My two previous first grade experiences did not meet the German requirements. The grammar school in Steinkirchen was within walking distance of our house. The impact of the war certainly was apparent in the schools. Normally in Germany the teachers were mostly men. But now older women were teaching school because men were fighting in the war and younger women were working in the war effort in other capacities. Class was held infrequently during the bombing raids. They did not want to gather the children during those dangerous times.

We had reading material and schoolwork that we had to do on our own during the bombing campaigns. Since paper was needed for the war effort, our homework was all done on a slate that was about a foot square. We had to protect it from the rain when we walked back to school because if it got wet, the homework would be washed off. Occasionally we had something that we could use for paint but we did not have paint brushes. The teacher was able to get us some horsehair to use for our brushes. We cut each hair into pieces about an inch long and then bound one end tightly. Then we gathered quills from the chickens. We cut each quill about four inches long and the teacher helped us glue the horsehair brushes into the end of the quill. I still have one of those brushes.

The school, like my grandparents' house, had outhouses, one for boys and one for girls. On the playground we played games, sang and danced. The school was small with three classrooms, one for each grade, first through third. Each child brought his own lunch because there was no lunchroom. In the classroom, rather than individual desks, we had tables for every two students. A cute little girl came and took the seat next to me at my table and she and I became friends. She sometimes came by our house to visit. She never came alone but always had a friend with her. I actually considered her my girlfriend and her friend a chaperone.

In first grade I studied math, music and what would be called social studies in America. I also had to learn to read and write Gothic German. This was especially helpful since my grandmother only wrote in Gothic. Eventually I finished my third, and last, year in first grade.

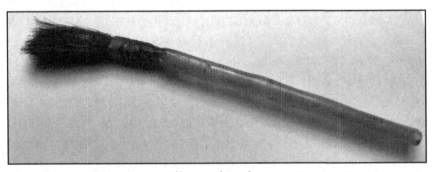

Horsehair and chicken quill paintbrush. Wesselhoeft collection

CHAPTER 11

The Bombings

From 1944 to 1945, the war was in full force in Germany. The Americans bombed in the daytime and the British at night. I suppose my grandparents had told my parents that the Allied Forces were bombing the area day and night. They also must have briefed them on what procedures they had worked out to try to stay safe during the bombings.

A warning system indicated how many minutes we had until the aircraft would reach our area. Very solid bomb shelters were everywhere. At night when the warning sounded, my mother would wake me. She had laid out my clothes and dressed me in everything I could possibly wear. We then went to the nearest bunker where we waited until the raid was over. When the raids started during the daytime, if I was outside I headed home and we would follow the same routine. We soon learned that people sometimes were trapped in the bunkers because the entrances got covered with bombing debris so we decided not to use them anymore. Because the attackers never changed their approach path, we used the time we had to move away from their path.

At times when we heard the siren warning, we would then see the sky absolutely full of aircraft coming more or less from the west. Airplanes seemed to fill the sky everywhere we looked!

They flew along the nearby Elbe River on their incoming bomb runs. We were directly under them. All along the levee of the Elbe anti-aircraft guns (triple-A) kept the air filled with puffs of black smoke. However, we did not hear the triple-A firing, bombs exploding, or any other noises of war, because the roar of the airplanes was so deafening that it drowned out all the other sounds. The massive presence of all those planes left an indelible impression on me. They seemed to be wingtip to wingtip from horizon to horizon. Finally, with relief, we would hear and see the planes going off into the distance.

While our suburb of Steinkirchen was not specifically a target, we were certainly not immune to the dangers. Airplanes that got hit would have to eject their bombs wherever they were, if they could. Fighters zipped in and out—some getting shot down. When fighter planes got hit, they jettisoned their tip tanks, fuel tanks on the tips of the wings, and those came down in our area. I actually got one of those tip tanks and later made a boat out of it.

Things crashed all over the place. One time a tip tank came down hitting a nearby house, catching it on fire. When a German warplane crashed and was not burned up, we took the tires off and cut them up to use for shoe soles. They did not wear out. The shoe upper might wear out but not the soles. Germany did not have rubber during the war, so they had to make an artificial rubber that they called *Buna*. This was used for all military aircraft and vehicle tires and it was practically indestructible.

During the daytime we watched the air battle. Sometimes B-17s and other airplanes would suddenly leave the formation and start tumbling down, losing wings and other parts as they fell. I expected more people to jump out of the planes but seldom saw a parachute open. I saw firsthand the horrors of war.

I really could not understand this warfare; I wondered why they had to bomb this city. I thought in war soldiers fought soldiers, a ground war so to speak, but yet the airplanes were bombing relentlessly. The ground was being destroyed and aircrews were obviously dying, all of it horrible to watch.

Fighter planes strafed the area around us, killing cattle and horses, which were vital to us all. When they killed livestock, people would recover the meat in order to have food. The bombers dropped chaff, strips of aluminum foil, to confuse the German anti-aircraft radar units as to the aircraft's exact altitude and flight path. This chaff filled the air and some of it fell on our property, which I picked up.

I also found a cylindrical device that was about a foot long and about four inches in diameter. My curiosity led me to take it apart and I found it loaded with flint stones. That led me to think it was an incendiary bomb that had not ignited. Later these flints were good for barter because they were used in cigarette lighters.

On one occasion my grandfather was up in an apple tree, I suppose trying to prune it. All of a sudden a German fighter plane, being chased by a P-38 with its guns blazing, came right over the top of him. My grandfather was knocked or fell out of the tree.

Opposite page, top. B 24 Liberator, 8th Air Force, blowing up a high octane plant in Hamburg
Opposite page, bottom. B 24 Liberator, 8th Air Force, bombing Hamburg area through heavy cloud cover and flak
Above. Destruction of buildings after 8th Air Force heavy bombing in Hamburg area, smoke still rising 25 hours later
Courtesy National Archives RG 342, Series FH US Air Force Photo Collection

I looked up and watched the chase. I then looked around on the ground for shells that I thought would surely be there because the planes were no more than ten feet over the top of the tree. I guess my grandfather was at least somewhat OK because he got right up and ran out of the way...albeit a bit too late. I don't even know if he knew I was around...it happened so quickly!

At night we could not see the airplanes but of course, we could hear their thunderous noise. Naturally we kept all lights out but the fires from incendiary bombs burned so brightly that we could read by them. My dad told me about the incendiary bombings in Hamburg where every day they picked up corpses of people who had shrunk like mummies because the fires consumed all the oxygen from the air. My dad

Above and opposite page. P-38 Like the one that "knocked" Wes' grandfather out of the apple tree.
Photo taken on Lackland AFB March 2018

had various jobs in the city of Hamburg. Of course, we never knew if he had survived the bombings or not until he returned home.

The bombing raids came in campaigns. Once started, they bombed every day and night for several days. Sometimes raids ended early because the fires were too intense to continue the mission, or the weather intervened and provided us with a reprieve.

I collected various types of ammunition. In a very short period of time, I learned a lot about guns and ammunition. I first learned about my grandfather's gun, called a drilling, which was a combination shot-gun and rifle. It had two barrels for birds and a third

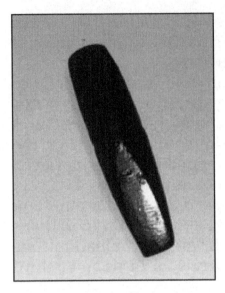

Bullet which Wes filed into a soldering tool

barrel for defense in case he came across a boar. The bullet for killing boar was just a plain lead bullet.

All the military ammunition that I collected had a copper jacket and I was curious what was inside. I used my grandfather's vice and filed the bullets in half lengthwise so I could see what was inside. I was surprised by the different types of construction. I wondered why they were different. Were some intended just to injure and others to kill? I still have those bullets but do not know the purpose of the different designs. Some of them that I found I thought were incendiaries containing phosphor.

At times my dad and I would take walks and look at the craters that were caused by bombers which had to jettison their bomb load. These were close by, within easy walking distance. We also visited the house that had been hit by a tip tank. The tank still had fuel in it that sprayed into the kitchen, catching it on fire.

I began having dreams at night that I believe were influenced by my interest in airplanes and flying as well as the futuristic comics I had been reading in Crystal City. In my dreams I was able to take a few steps, flap my arms, and fly away from the stress of the war. I only had these dreams when we were in Steinkirchen and were experiencing the bombings.

Steinkirchen. Wes found these bullets and filed them in half to see what was inside.

In less than a year's time my world had totally changed. I started as a little American boy in Chicago, where I rode bikes and played hide-and-seek. Then we were taken to Crystal City, where I was fascinated with the snakes and spiders and picked up pretty rocks that I thought were meteorites in a world so quiet I could hear only the woodworking shop nearby. Then I was in Germany, still an American boy, with the deafening roar of Allied airplanes overhead filling the sky and bombing all around me. Instead of pretty rocks, I picked up chaff, stray ammunition and what I thought were incendiary bombs. Instead of taking apart alarm clocks, I filed military ammunition apart to see what was inside. Instead of collecting baby snakes in my pocket, I collected flints from incendiary bombs that were bartered for family necessities.

CHAPTER 12

On the Move Again

Gross Quasdow, Pommern. At some point, my mother and I went to live with her mother in Gross Quasdow, Pommern, on the Baltic Sea close to Schlawe. This was in the eastern part of north Germany which is now Poland. We lived there with my grandmother, my uncle Karl and his two sons about my age. My cousins and I spent our time playing together. I did not attend school while we were there.

We lived in the home my mother grew up in, a typical farmhouse. We had cows, pigs, chickens and a horse and wagon, as well as a field where they grew some type of crop. While we were there, my grand-mother taught me to pray every night when I went to bed. We did not have an abundance of food but it was adequate. The people there were very self-sufficient.

This area was isolated from the war and usually pleasant and very quiet. However, once a Russian fighter shot down a German bomber and the bomber crashed nearby in a field. Only one parachute came down from the German bomber but it landed right in the burning aircraft. Everyone around came out and just stood watching the plane burn. There was nothing they could do. Then the officials came and sent everyone away.

On one occasion, Uncle Karl hitched up the horse and wagon so that we could all go on an outing into Schlawe for a bit of shopping for goods we needed. It was not a very long trip. I found it memorable because I had never taken a trip in an open, horse-drawn wagon. Going to Steinkirchen from America was a step back in time in itself, but this area seemed to be even farther yet.

The people there used *torf*, called peat in English, as fuel for heat. The men would cut the thick decaying vegetable matter from marshy land into bricks about twice the size of a house brick and lay it in the field to dry in the sun. As a young girl, my mother's job was to haul it in a wheelbarrow back to the house. She said it was very heavy and hard work. Torf burned rather quickly, so I imagine they needed quite a supply.

The people lived and worked closely together. The farmhouses were fairly close to one another with their fields in the outlying area. They had a community oven in the middle of the village which was kept burning all the time. Each family had a designated time for baking their bread. Once baked, the bread was stored in a wooden chest until their next turn. The bread was very heavy and dark and could be kept for weeks. The outside was crusty but the inside remained soft.

We stayed there with my grandmother until we heard that the Russians were moving into the area. We did not want to fall under Russian control because we had heard horrible stories of what it was like when the "Red Army" moved in. My mother decided that she and I would go back to Steinkirchen even though living there had been very hard.

We moved back into my grandparents' home, into the room where we had lived before. My father was still working anywhere he could get work, the bombings were still going on, and school was still intermittent.

CHAPTER 13

Severe Winter

Hamburg/Steinkirchen, Winter 1944. The winter of 1944–45 was especially cold. I did not know it at the time but this was the winter of the famous Battle of the Bulge. Many Americans know of the extremely harsh winter our soldiers endured while fighting this difficult and significant battle. It was the harshest winter I experienced in all the years I lived in Germany. Luckily my dad had bought me some good winter clothes in Lisbon. Coal for heating was not available to us and neither was wood except for roots of trees that had been destroyed by bombing or burning. As a child I helped cut those roots and it was very hard work.

The ditches that normally flowed into the river were frozen, often down to the ground. The Luhe River actually froze in spite of the movement caused by the tide going up and down. When the tide went out and the ice was suspended in the air, my friends and I, or even I alone, would go out on the ice and bounce on it to get it to crack. When it cracked, it made a deafening sound as the crack ran up and down the river. If it was cold enough at night, it would freeze over again and we could have our fun another day.

We went ice skating on the ditches and could go for miles from one ditch to the other. The skates were the type that clamped onto the soles of our shoes, much like roller skates were in those days in the US. We also had one-person ice sleds which had steel bands along the bottom edges that glided like ice skates on the ice. We used long sticks held in each hand, kind of like ski poles with sharp metal pins on the end, to push the sled along the ice to travel on the frozen ditches.

The roads were also frozen over. Every once in a while a car came by, moving very slowly. We boys would lie in wait with a rope tied to our sled. We would try to catch our rope on to the bumper of the car so it would tow us along for a while. We didn't want to go through the main part of the village, so before we got there, we let go. Usually the rope just came loose from the bumper, but once in a while it caught on the car and the sled would go tumbling from side to side behind the car. If it did not come off, we just lost that sled. When that happened, we boys took off running for home, not wanting to claim our sled or the mischief we had unintentionally created. We knew that once the car got into the more populated part of the village the sled would surely end up with the police. In Germany at that time no one wanted to attract the attention of the authorities. As much fun as we had playing with our sled, we were much more afraid of the police than concerned about the loss of a toy.

CHAPTER 14

Toward the End of the War

As the war raged on, anything that could support the war effort was either unavailable or rationed, including food items. Everything was scarce and many shelves were empty. Although we were still able to get most necessities we had to barter for them. Like most people, we grew a garden and fruit trees. We had one apple tree that we did not barter out. It grew right by the house and was called a Cox-orange. It produced a really ugly apple with wart-like things on it but they were the best tasting apples we had.

Coffee was very important to the German people but during the war regular coffee was nearly impossible to come by. People made coffee from acorns, walnuts, and just about anything. This was called *Ersatz*, which means substitute, a word that not only applied to coffee. Other substitutes included ersatz rubber and ersatz oil. The government made many items from coal, which was primarily reserved for the war industry and was severely rationed for the people.

More and more people roamed the streets looking for shelter because their homes had been bombed out. They also were looking for food. Although we did not have much, my family always seemed to have a little bit, so we would give people that came by at least a little something to eat.

At one time a family member whose home had been bombed out in Hamburg came to my grandparents looking for a place to live. They ended up in the property next to ours, living in the grain mill. The mill was a very large building with living quarters that under normal operation would have been occupied by mill workers. This mill was run from time to time to keep it functioning, but it never seemed to be used for grain.

Every family who had any space for a bed had to take people in. Eventually a couple came and lived in the small room on the front of my grandparents' bedroom which had just barely enough room for a bed. They lived with us in that little room for about a year or so. Now this small one-family home actually housed three families. Eventually the couple found another place to stay and asked my family what they might do to show their gratitude. The man was a tailor so they suggested that he make a suit for me. Somehow he got some nice wool and made a beautiful tailored suit for me. In Chicago my mother liked to dress in the latest fashions and always liked to dress me up to look really nice. She was so proud for people to see me in that suit.

One day I was out playing in my new suit. My friends and I climbed up in a neighbor's walnut tree, which was loaded with walnuts, and helped ourselves to the fruit. My new suit had lots of pockets which I stuffed with the nuts. One of the kids from the owner's family came by on horseback, probably knowing we were there. We quickly got out of the tree and I stretched out on the ground by the side of the drainage ditch. Luckily he didn't see me because I was so flat on the ground by the ditch—with pockets that were full of walnuts! The husks on the walnuts have a fluid in them that will stain clothing. When I finally stood up, my pockets were wet and my new, pretty suit was ruined.

Gypsies began moving through our village with donkeys that pulled their small house trailers. They roamed onto people's property and stole the chickens, eggs, or anything else of value for barter or living. We had to keep an eye out for them and make a visible presence so they did not take anything from our property. I didn't even know gypsies existed in Germany and had never encountered them before. People seemed to think they were more of a threat than the people who came by asking for a place to stay or for some food.

We had no paper at all toward the end of and after the war. If a book had a blank page, we took it out and used it for paper. The rest of the book would go into the outhouse for toilet paper. Our family library ended up as toilet paper. Books hung from a hook on the wall in the outhouse. One day I found a book of German songs that I took from the outhouse. I kept that book and still have it today.

Another book that was *mostly* saved from the outhouse was my grandfather's navigation guide. He had begun as a sailmaker—I still have the sewing palm that he used to sew sails. He worked his way up to a navigator on sailing ships. He took a course in celestial navigation and had his mathematical notes including how to get a position from the sun, moon, planets, and stars, all written out with excellent penmanship in a big beautiful book. I still have that book with its missing pages that were used either as writing paper or toilet paper. I have no idea what significant information might have been lost from that book.

We also had a family Bible that was printed in Stade under permission of the Swedish king in 1702. The Swedes were occupying Germany at the time. I have the family Bible and fortunately no pages are missing. I guess the family just would not use the Bible for toilet paper.

Late in the war, to stop the advance of the Allies, the Germans blew up the bridges crossing the Luhe River. They blew up the one right in the middle of Steinkirchen. The effect of this was more detrimental to the villagers than the Allies. It left the people on the east side of Steinkirchen isolated from all the facilities in the village. But naturally it did not stop the Allies' movement toward Hamburg.

CHAPTER 15

The Hitler Youth

During the war the Hitler Youth was active in Steinkirchen and other nearby villages. It, like everything else in socialist Germany, was created by and for the government. So its connection to the Nazis was no surprise. The Hitler Youth was mandatory for boys age ten and up.

Although the primary purpose was indoctrination and to prepare the young men to be soldiers, many of the programs were very educational. The boys had shooting competitions with some sort of weapons provided. Tanks light enough for our roads were brought in so they could experience riding in them. They also learned to fly in gliders. Of course that part seemed exciting to me since I had already had an interest in airplanes.

I heard older boys talking with great enthusiasm about all the interesting things they were doing. What boy would not be interested in such things as outdoor skills, sports, competition, and riding in a tank? For me especially flying in a glider sounded like real fun! Naturally those kinds of activities without the Nazi propaganda and war emphasis would be fascinating to almost any boy; they counted on that in fact.

Except for the paramilitary aspect, the Hitler Youth was much like Explorer Scout training. Boys learned an assortment of skills, especially regarding outdoor living. Like the scouts, they received badges for all their accomplishments. They trained in survival skills, such as how to kill and cook whatever food might be available. Physical fitness was also important. Periodically, they marched down the street in formation with their fife and drums, wearing their proper uniforms including, of course, their brown shirts, looking very sharp and smart! One could not help but notice them. They were a real presence.

The girl counterpart to the Hitler Youth wore uniforms similar to the Girl Scouts. These girls took younger boys on nature walks and taught the boys songs and lessons about nature.

Hitler Youth from nearby villages would compete in games where each group had its own territory and the others tried to conquer it, a type of kid's war game. One group would try to sneak up on the other group and conquer their headquarters. The game was not just strategic; it was also physical as one group defended their territory and the other tried to penetrate those defenses. They sometimes got pretty rough in these games, using sticks to hit one another.

Thankfully, I was too young for the mandatory Hitler Youth. I had no inclination to align myself with those philosophies. I, being an American boy, would never have joined. I shudder to think what the outcome would have been had I been within the mandatory age. Where might I have ended up?

As the war went on and things got worse and worse, the Hitler Youth lost some of its charm to boys as the government took younger and younger men into the war. Now young boys with their fife and drums and uniforms actually faced the harsh reality of going to war. They were probably further demoralized by the constant aerial bombings and scenes of destruction in Hamburg. More and more disabled ships lined the banks of the Elbe River.

Hamburg streets after the war, showing effects of bombing
NARA RG 342, Series FH US Air Force Photo Collection

CHAPTER 16

War Ends

The Allied bombing of Hamburg had been very successful. The city was destroyed. I later heard it referred to as the Hiroshima of Germany. Of course, Hamburg was but one city that was so ruined. Sometime later I also heard that the Allies intended to leave not one brick standing on another in Germany. They were pretty successful with that effort.

I first knew that the war was over when I saw Allied military men driving through Steinkirchen. Scottish soldiers drove by me sitting on the hood of the vehicles cleaning their guns. I later learned we were in the British Occupation Zone.

The troops came in and were all over the area up and down the Luhe River. They commandeered buildings for maintaining their trucks, tanks, and other equipment.

I went over and watched them doing maintenance on trucks and other vehicles. I also watched them line up the troops and inspect them. They were all in a single row wearing their kilts. The guy doing the inspecting had a mirror on the toe of his boot. The troops were then released to go into town. Naturally, they were looking for entertainment.

Our friends with older brothers soon realized that things had changed in their lives. The soldiers that now occupied the area had food, clothes, nylons, cigarettes, and money. This left the German boys, who had nothing, out in the cold with the girls. The soldiers had plenty. I watched as the soldiers smoked a cigarette, dropped it in the mud, and smashed it out; then Germans would fight over the tobacco in the mud. It was common to see people under blankets and even a young child could figure out what was going on. We soon began seeing "balloons" lying on the side of the road.

Those were the initial things we saw of the occupation. But the postwar reality was we still had to find a way to survive. The years after the war were very, very hard, actually worse than during it. Our food and other necessities were already limited. It is hard to imagine, but when the war was over, even less was available. All the production and industry, in fact the whole economy, was completely shut down in Germany. The factories were dismantled. People did not have even the basic necessities of life. Instead of toothpaste we used salt. We had no soap, food, toilet paper—nothing. But the number one thing in demand was food. People were starving and many were homeless after the war. Some of my friends who lived on farms with milk cows also grew sugar beets for the cows. They would give me some of the sugar beets which I thought were very good cooked or raw.

The soldiers controlled everything. The river and roads all had checkpoints. The only way to survive was to depend on the illegal underground black market. The occupation forces issued some kind of "funny money" but it was just that, useless because there was nothing to buy.

My family had only what we could harvest from our fruit trees and garden. In the garden we mainly grew beans. We prepared the beans for canning, put them in unsealed cans and took them right away to the local bicycle shop. I do not know where the cans came from. The local bicycle shop had equipment to commercially seal vegetable cans. We then would use those cans of beans and our fruit for barter.

The difficult part was getting our limited goods to Hamburg with its big black market. There they could be bartered for other things we needed. But of course, to get to Hamburg, we had to get past the British control points. My dad managed to get a sailboat which he used as a rowboat. He took advantage of the weather, the tides, fog, wind, and darkness to float past the checkpoints undetected. He would go and barter for the things we needed. He never got caught. Bartering was a way to stay alive in post-war Germany.

We never wanted to get meat from Hamburg. We all knew a can of meat from there might be anything. I don't know where we got meat, but whatever meat we got was very tough and it didn't matter how long it was boiled; it was still tough. It was the same with chickens; they were not used for meat until they quit laying eggs. They had to be old and worn out!

Eventually everything was traded, even my things. My American bicycle was one of the first of my things to go. I also had a steam factory system, a platform that housed a steam-generating tank. The steam it created then drove the various attachments. I really enjoyed that toy, but it too got bartered.

An album that meant a lot to me was another treasure that ended up being bartered. During the time when we could still buy food in Germany, companies had a marketing technique to create customer loyalty. They produced an album with stories in it, which could be bought for one Mark. With the additional purchase of that company's product, the customer would receive a little picture that related to one of the stories. The little picture was meant to be put in the album next to the relevant story. I had one of those albums that was about life in the Middle Ages—how a dentist pulled teeth, how medical practices like leeching were performed, how carpenters worked. I really liked that album and I wish I could have kept it.

At some point three families were living in my great-grandfather's house. One family were refugees from the East. The man raised rabbits for their meat supply. He gave me a baby rabbit to have for a pet; I suppose he was confident there would be more. I made a cage by the chicken coop and somehow found a bit of food, grass, or whatever to feed my pet rabbit. He or she, whichever it was, grew to be adult-sized. Well, one day when I went out to see about it, the door was open and it was gone. The story was it must have somehow escaped. I never wanted to know which meal that might have been.

After the war, rats became a huge problem. They were just everywhere. The village put poison around to try to eradicate them. Unfortunately our family cat, Budabu, ate one of the poisoned rats and he died an awful death that night. We kids had a way to deal with the rodents. We would take a pole with a net on the end and try to catch one. If we caught a rat we would then hold it under the water until it drowned. We also shot them. Some kids had 22s or air rifles that they used for this.

People who still owned guns had them confiscated by the occupation forces. Hitler had required that all guns be registered as a "safety measure" for his people. When the occupation forces came in, they just had to go to the Rathouse (city hall), get the list of who had what guns and go to the people and collect them. My grandfather had his J.P. Sauer drilling shotgun and also had two dueling pistols. The British took all three, so I imagine that someone in Britain has some very nice guns today.

Now that my grandfather did not have a gun to keep the starlings away, we had to use noisemakers. We used "carbide cannons," which sounded just like a gun. These were a lot of trouble to use but we needed to protect our fruit any way we could. The cannon was a canister that used carbide gas which was ignited with a spark. This blew the lid off the canister and sounded like a gun. It was minimally effective in chasing away the birds but did not provide starlings to eat which my grandfather had been able to do with his drilling shotgun.

My grandfather and his survival skills had been very valuable to the family during and after the war. Sadly, he became ill and was diagnosed with throat cancer. They put a bed in the Gute Stube and that's where he stayed until he passed away. I think he was pretty uncomfortable and he wanted things to be very quiet. My friends and I tried to be quiet but I think we did not succeed. He was treated by a doctor who had an office in the village and also made house calls. This probably helped keep illnesses from spreading.

About a year or so after the war ended, each month when my dad came home from Hamburg, he brought an honest-to-goodness CARE (the Cooperative for Assistance and Relief to Europe) package which we anticipated and greatly appreciated. My dad told me that it came to me from the Consulate because I was an American citizen. This CARE package contained much-needed items such as flour, sugar, soap, and other items for hygiene. We used the things that were absolutely essential for our family and bartered the other items. I was pleased that I was able to help out with these things that were so priceless. For my part I did claim the little can of sweetened condensed milk. This was my only candy. That I was an American child, exchanged into a horrific war zone and now receiving a monthly CARE package from the US was, in retrospect, too ironic to believe.

On one occasion when my dad came with the CARE package, he also brought me a pair of boots from the military surplus store. The boots had soles that had some kind of metal spikes in them. I did not know if this was to make them more durable or to provide traction in the snow. But I really liked those boots because of the sound they made when I walked on the cobblestone streets. They were really too big for me and I had to wear several pairs of socks with them. Eventually, I grew into them and even wore them out, but they served me well for several winters.

I saw my very first movie in Steinkirchen. Of course, it was an American film. The village did not have a movie theater, but on one occasion someone set up a movie projector and sound system in a community center. I have no idea where the equipment or even the movie came from, perhaps the soldiers. My mother took me there and we saw *Gone with the Wind*.

Accustomed as I was to war, that part of the film did not affect me. I was more impressed by the rural Southern way of life with their plantations and elaborate clothes. This period of American history was new to me. I think my mother wanted to take this opportunity to show me something of America. Even though it was not the America we had left behind, it was as close as she could get.

During the occupation we were able to have school regularly, except for the time when we were evacuated from the school building because the bunkers were going to be destroyed. We all were excited and anticipated the big moment when the bunker would be blown up. What could be more fun! Supposedly the soldiers had loaded the bunker with sufficient explosives to destroy it. But instead, when the big moment came, the lid of the bunker just lifted a tiny bit off its foundation and then settled back down in a cloud of smoke. We found this quite a funny sight and we all laughed and talked about it as we went back to school.

Now that the war was over, carnivals traveled around from town to town. I found out I could help assemble the carousel and earn free tickets to ride. On one occasion I thought it would be a good idea to use all my tickets at once and just stay on the carousel for a good long ride around and around. When I got off, I was disoriented and sick as a dog! I never did that again. I didn't really want to ever see a carousel again.

With the war over, the North Sea was once again accessible. It had been heavily mined at the entrance of the Elbe to prevent the German U-boats and other war ships from entering the North Sea. The Allies had successfully prevented warships from going into the North Sea, but fishing boats as well had no access to their traditional fishing grounds. Now that the mines were finally removed, the fishing boats were again free to go out into the North Sea to ply their trade. Because the waters had not been fished for so long, the fishermen hauled in blockbuster catches of huge fish. They brought in flounders that were at least four feet long and six inches thick, the likes of which had not been seen in many years.

I learned a few valuable lessons living in Germany during the war and the following years. I learned to eat whatever was available. I also learned that everything had a use; therefore everything had to be saved. No matter what it was, anything could be used, bartered, or altered in some way to help us survive.

Life was very difficult in Germany until the Marshall Plan went into effect in 1948 and things began to improve.

CHAPTER 17

The Gymnasium

I attended school in Steinkirchen from 1944 to 1947. I lost one whole year because of the bombing. In Germany the standard school system is twelve grades, much as it is in America. One big difference is that students have to decide at an early age whether they want to pursue a university education or go into a trade. At age eleven, students who are interested in going on to higher education have to take and pass a test to attend the Gymnasium for college preparation. The test to get in to the Gymnasium is very difficult. I suppose my three years in first grade helped because I passed.

The attrition rate is also very high because the courses are quite challenging. The teachers, unlike in the schools during the war years, were all men who had advanced degrees. Many had a Ph.D. In Germany finishing the Gymnasium is prestigious, and also necessary in order to go on to a university to become a doctor, lawyer, or for any other profession. Each Gymnasium specialized in certain disciplines. The ones I attended focused on science and modern languages.

At the Gymnasium from time to time some farm kids who were attending had a bit of extra food and put it on the teacher's desk before class. Supposedly no one knew which student had brought the food.

In 1948, I entered Athenaeum Gymnasium in Stade, which was about ten miles away, the same city where our family Bible was printed in 1702. I traveled to school on a bus. I had to get up very early, leave while it was still dark, spend the day in school, and then go back home in the evening.

On the way to school one morning, I was sitting over the right rear dual-tire wheel well when all of a sudden I felt something funny under me. The bus kind of settled as if it were sinking into a soft down pillow. I looked out the window and a pair of tires was running down the road right alongside the bus. The bus slowed down; the tires continued on at the same speed. The driver stopped the bus and went for help. So for that day there was no school for us. We students naturally had a really good time with the whole affair.

All Gymnasiums have religious training. The instructor that we had was not of any particular denomination. He taught us a good concept of God and Christ, not from the perspective of any particular doctrine. This was my first exposure to the idea that there is another approach to religion besides just Catholic and Lutheran.

My parents had to pay for me to attend the Gymnasium although public school was free. I attended that Gymnasium in Stade until 1950.

CHAPTER 18

Move to Konstanz

Konstanz, 1950. In 1950, We decided to move to Konstanz, in the French zone, because the area had not been bombed out during the war. The city is beautiful and right on the Swiss border. The Allies could not distinguish it from the Swiss side and this had provided enough protection that the people living there did not have to have blackouts at night. It sits on the picturesque Lake Konstanz, the beginning of the Rhine River.

Soon after arriving in Konstanz, I was surprised to be called into the police station. Sometime during the late '40s before we moved to Konstanz, I was playing with my friend who had an air rifle. We were shooting at a target on one of those icy ditches. One of the bullets ricocheted off the ice and hit a pedestrian in the neck. He was quite far away and we did not even know it happened. But he called the police and they came and took the report, which followed me to Konstanz when I moved there. Ah, the German *Ausweis*—every German had one and everything you had ever done was in there, The police kept track of every person—their whereabouts, their source of employment, and their vacations. While I did not have a German *Auswies* they still kept track of everything I did including this mishap. Thankfully they did not know about me and my sled.

I transferred to the Humboldt Gymnasium in Konstanz. Besides the rigorous math, science and language classes, a dance class was mandatory. Traditionally, every year in a certain grade, we would learn ballroom dancing. The boys' Gymnasium would dance with the girls from the girls' Gymnasium who were one year younger. They told us that this was so we could help them with their homework. We learned the waltz, foxtrot and tango at a local dance school.

In Konstanz the population was about equally divided between Catholic and Protestant. In addition to our other academic classes, we had religious education and unlike the Gymnasium in Stade, the students went either to Catholic or to Lutheran class. All other classes were held together and we had some pretty provocative conversations about religion. Although it troubled me that the Christian body was divided this way, I pretty much embraced the Lutheran teaching.

After moving to Konstanz, my dad insisted that we all go to church. He selected Die Paulus Kirche which was Lutheran. I had a good friend who also attended that church. We were part of the youth group and as such had certain responsibilities. He and I were selected to pump the bellows for the church organ. During one particular church service while we were pumping the bellows, we looked into each other's eyes and we had the same idea at once. We both let go of the pump handles and the church organ died with a mournful sound! We didn't have that job any more.

I was confirmed in that church at the age of fourteen through the ceremony of the Lord's Supper. At this point I was considered a Christian in the Lutheran Church. I attended Die Paulus Kirche the entire time I lived in Konstanz. I did a lot of Bible reading during that time. The teaching in the Gymnasium and at church, along with my own independent Bible study, had at least two important effects on me. It developed a deeper foundation for my religion and at the same time raised a lot of unanswered questions. I continued to believe in God and Jesus. I never doubted that God has a plan and is in charge of all things.

Postcard from Konstanz

Wes on hike to Norway

CHAPTER 19

Our Trip to Norway

Norway. By this time the Hitler Youth no longer existed and young boys joined the more internationally known Boy Scouts. This was something I could be and was a part of. I enjoyed my time in the Boy Scouts and we learned a lot. A local man donated an old, old castle to our troop. The abandoned castle sat on an extinct volcano to the west of Konstanz. We worked to fix it up and made it usable as a Scout building. This castle was the challenge that we took on to learn how they had lived back in earlier days.

In the summer of 1957, three of us from our troop took a trip to Sweden and Norway. We just wanted to go to the Arctic Circle. The three of us met up in northern Germany to start our journey. Each of us got to our meeting point independently. We then went up the east side through Sweden and came down the Norwegian side on the west.

We hitchhiked and walked the whole way. Sometimes when people picked us up, they asked for a small donation to help with the gas. Often someone stopped without enough room in the vehicle for all three of us. Sometimes they only had room for one, so we would get split up. We leapfrogged our way to a predetermined city on our agenda where we planned to reconnect.

This trip provided some interesting experiences for me. At one point I was walking around alone in Stockholm and noticed an amusement park that looked intriguing. A family saw me at the gate. They could not help noticing that I was wearing my scout uniform and carrying my backpack and guitar. They invited me to go into the park with them. They paid my way and we spent a couple of enjoyable hours there together.

Another time when I was alone, a man in a BIG American Ford picked me up. He was really proud of this car and its power. I am not sure how fast he was going, but he let it rip. Compared to the small European cars, this one was huge. It seemed as if I was sitting a long way from the driver on the other side. He invited me to go with him to visit his mother and to stay the night with them. Their toilet reminded me of ours in Steinkirchen, but everything went down a very long slope; by the time it got to the bottom, which took quite some time, it had converted to compost. They used it in their garden. His mother was very welcoming and hospitable to me. Before I went on my way, she served me an American breakfast of Kellogg's Corn Flakes and milk.

At one point, I was hitchhiking alone in the pouring rain someplace in Norway. Luckily a guy stopped to pick me up. The windshield wipers were not working on his car, so as we drove along, I had to reach out the window and operate the windshield wipers manually. I am sure he picked me up because he needed the help, which all in all was a win-win situation.

On another occasion when all three of us were to-gether, a couple picked us up because they saw my guitar and wanted to hear some songs. So with the three of us in the backseat of the car, I played the guitar and we sang German Boy Scout songs as we drove along.

On one occasion when being separated we planned a rendezvous in a certain town but foolishly had not designated a precise place to meet up. I got a ride there and then found a public restroom. While in the restroom, who walked in but one of my travel companions! Now all we had to do was find the third friend, which we eventually did.

The further north we went the smaller the trees got. A funny thing about those trees was we could break off a branch and it would burn even though the tree was green. Eventually instead of trees some kind of ankle-high mossy vegetation grew.

Shopping for our supplies was not a problem because the people spoke English or German. All three of us had at least some English training. Most nights my friends and I spent outdoors. We had hammocks that we tied between trees, where there were trees. We had a cover in case it rained. It was summer time but still chilly. We took our baths in rivers or lakes. One time we were actually skinny-dipping and some people came along; because I was naked I had to wait in the cold water until they moved on. One thing we noticed was that the Norwegian soldiers were always maneuvering. Here we were hitchhiking and walking while the military men were running in full field gear. They were in excellent physical condition, much like our Marines.

The Norwegians used a different measure for distance. We soon learned, for example, a couple of "clicks" (slang for kilometer) was not a couple of kilometers as we knew it. Instead a click was actually ten kilometers. So a "couple of clicks" meant twenty kilometers rather than two, important information for us to have. The roads zigzagged along the fjords west and east with little north or south movement. So we traveled quite a few clicks without moving very far north or south. I guessed this was why they measured things differently than in Germany.

We went all the way to Tromso, which is about 200 miles north of the Arctic Circle. Around the Arctic Circle area everything was foggy, grey, and rainy. The school kids wore raincoats in very bright colors—bright reds and yellow—the only color to the place.

Somewhere in this far northern part of Norway we met a local guy who invited us to his home for the night. This gave us an opportunity to learn a bit about how the people lived up there. He did not have a garden but had a herd of reindeer that he used for food.

The three of us considered that we made that trip together; in our own way we actually did, though sometimes we were together and sometimes we were not. Somehow we did all end up together back in northern Germany. Then each began his trip back south to Konstanz.

CHAPTER 20

The Story of "Old Joe"

Our rendezvous point in northern Germany from which we launched our Norway trip was the home of friends of one of my three travel companions. To get there, I drove my motorcycle, "Old Joe." Old Joe had already lived a full life before I ever bought it. But it had a second life with me.

Old Joe was a thing in a class by itself! It had a two-cycle engine, a Sachs motor made in the Eastern part of Germany. I painted "Old Joe" on the fuel tank. It was not a full motorcycle because I could also pedal it. In fact, this is how I got it started. I would pedal it until I got enough speed and could start the engine. I had to prepare Old Joe for this trip from the most southern part of Germany to the very most northern part, checking it over really well.

At the time we were living in town on Rosgartenstrasse 31, where we had just a small room. Kind of like our room in Crystal City, it was about ten by twenty feet with three beds, a table, a coal burning stove, a closet, and a window out back. There were five other apartments and a community kitchen.

I kept the motorcycle in the backyard. I started taking the engine apart and taking it up to the room where I worked on it. I replaced the compression rings on the engine piston and put the engine back together. I also checked the wheel bearings, making sure they were clean and greased. I got it as roadworthy as I could. I then had to pass the driving test and get a driver's license. I was able to pass the test with no problem.

I set out from Konstanz, got to the edge of the town, and then the thing quit! I soon figured out what the problem was. The spark plug was fouled. A two-cycle engine uses a spark plug designed for a gas and oil mixture. I did not know enough about matching the spark plug to the fuel/oil mixture. I had three spare spark plugs, so I put in a new spark plug and got it going again. I cleaned the first plug that had gotten fouled. The second spark plug ran for a while and

Old Joe

then it quit. Each time I would replace the plug from my three clean ones I had in reserve. In this process I learned which plugs ran best going uphill, downhill, or on flat land. Each had its own characteristic. I spent several days getting to northern Germany and along the way I stayed at youth hostels. At first this was a problem because they only allowed people traveling by foot or bicycle to stay there. But now, Old Joe was neither a bicycle nor a motorcycle, so they just let me stay. Another of the students in my class in Konstanz lived on my route to northern Germany and told me to stop and visit with him on the way up and back. Although he was not one of our group going to Norway, he said that if I would stop on the way back he would ride with me to Konstanz on his Vespa. On the way up I stopped and spent a couple of days with them. His dad was a very intimidating big, husky Paul Bunyan type. He was a forester in a local national park, Die Lueneburger Heide. He told me very emphatically that when I got to Norway, I had to be sure to visit the cemetery where the German soldiers were buried.

From their home I went on to our rendezvous place in northern Germany. While we were in Sweden and Norway, Old Joe stayed there at the home of the friends of one of my travel companions.

When we came back I picked up Old Joe and the whole thing started over again. I traveled back to Konstanz—one spark plug at a time.

However, on the return trip I did not have the nerve to stop back at my friend's home. I had not made an effort to find the German cemetery that his father had so emphatically instructed me to do. I decided to pass by and get back to Konstanz. But a family member saw me going through town and told the family they had seen me. My classmate did not drive his Vespa back; he went some other way. The whole affair was a bit awkward.

For protection from the weather I had a poncho over my body with my hands sticking out to hold on to the handlebars. I could only go forty kilometers per hour, which was the minimum autobahn speed. I ran into rainy weather several times. One day I was going through the Ruhr Gebiet, an industrial area of Germany. The autobahn was wet and slippery. I was having trouble keeping Old Joe on the road. Coming up behind me was an eighteen-wheeler type truck. He was trying somewhat unsuccessfully to slow down; he could see I was a bit out of control. I finally got off the autobahn and the truck missed me. Fortunately, this was my only scary situation on my ride with Old Joe. I just kept changing the spark plug and made it back home.

I sold Old Joe to someone and sometime later I was told that he was still running on the roads of Konstanz.

CHAPTER 21

Activities in Konstanz

Konstanz. Traveling carnivals came to Konstanz like they had done in Steinkirchen. At these carnivals vendors sold soaps and other items. The setup was quite simple with just a table, rain protection, their wares, and loud voices. The funny thing about it was they sounded just like the infomercials that I heard once I came back to the US and had television. The pitch was exactly the same, down to "...but wait! That's not all!" You would get one free or get some other thing that could be used in the kitchen. If the audience happened to be men, it might be tools or razors—buy this and get something else for free. Besides the fun, I enjoyed going to the carnivals in Konstanz because they always played Elvis music which I really liked.

In Konstanz I joined a rowing team on the Rhine River where it comes out of the *Bodensee* and goes into what is called the *Untersee*, a lake with beautiful swans and other wildlife. I had the number one seat right in the front of the rowing boat. Of course this position got the water spray. On a four-man boat the rowing seats were numbered 1 to 4. Number 5 counted the cadence and steered the boat and he could control the speed of the boat by his cadence. This was a great opportunity to see this part of the lake which was not accessible except by water.

Konstanz also had a mandolin orchestra with older experienced musicians. However, the orchestra needed more guitar players. The leader of the orchestra put out ads offering a free instruction class. From the attendees of the class he selected people to join his orchestra. Since I already owned a guitar but had no formal training, I took the class and was selected to be in the mandolin orchestra. In addition to conducting the orchestra, the leader gave private lessons for a small fee. I had a lot of private guitar lessons with him.

Konstanz also had a couple of factories so my friend and I went to one of the factories and applied to work during a month-long break from school. This particular factory was dyeing cloth. I got a job and was learning the dyeing process. I was only allowed to work with one type of fabric and one color. I had to run the cloth through various vats with chemical agents to get the right shade and evenness of color. The factories were looking for future employees, so they hired students. This job gave me enough money to buy a better guitar.

The number one mandolin player in the orchestra also had a mandolin and guitar store in town. Violin makers in Switzerland made most of his beautiful instruments. I went to see him about getting a better guitar for the orchestra. He helped me make a selection based on the money I had.

Playing in the mandolin orchestra was a nice reprieve from the stress of the Gymnasium. The guitar I bought to play in the orchestra was the one that came with me to the US on board the *SS Ryndam*. That guitar has brought me many pleasant hours of music.

CHAPTER 22

Black Powder

From chemistry classes in the Gymnasium, a couple of us got interested in black powder. I went to the pharmacy and bought the ingredients for us to make some on our own. I knew the exact proportions and the method to mix it.

In the room we had on Rosgartenstrasse, we had one table which my mother kept covered with a nice clean, white tablecloth. On that table, I started mixing the ingredients. I mixed the ingredients in a fairly large bowl.

I naturally had to test it to see if it would "work." I wisely put a sample into a little bowl before I put a match to it. However, one tiny little spark flew out of the little bowl, and as luck would have it, it headed straight for that big bowl of powder!

Now I had a big problem. Not only does black powder burn and spark, but it also creates a lot of smoke. The sparks burned through the tablecloth and into the table and the room filled with smoke.

I had to move fast because my dad would be coming home soon. Also, I was concerned about the other people living on that floor. I opened the window and the door to get a draft and used a towel to try to fan the smoke out of the room. I managed to get most of the smoke out, but sparks burned the table and tablecloth. I replaced the tablecloth. When my dad came home, he knew that something had happened, but he never knew the full extent of it.

With our newfound knowledge, my friends and I decided we would make firecrackers. We got small paper tubes which we packed with powder. We used a match as a fuse. We could light the match and it would burn down and set the black powder off. Every summer the Swiss and Germans had a joint festival with a huge fireworks display over the water. People came from all over to see the fireworks. Because this was quite a big attraction, during the festival we could get away with these firecrackers in the neighborhood, much like people shoot firecrackers in their neighborhood on Independence Day in America.

CHAPTER 23

Mother

While we were living in Konstanz, my mother became very ill. She had been diagnosed with breast cancer when we lived in Steinkirchen and after surgery had been declared cured. But the cancer returned with a vengeance; now it was all over her body. She spent a long time in the hospital. I was attending the Gymnasium, but every afternoon that I possibly could I visited her in the hospital and tried to do my homework at the same time. She was in a private room and we did talk some.

This was a particularly difficult time for me because I was naturally concerned about my mother. But I also had to study for my final exams at the Gymnasium. During that time I had trouble eating and all I could keep down was boiled, strained oatmeal. The doctor said I was developing an ulcer and recommended I eat licorice which was known to be good for the stomach.

My mother grew worse until she could only drink wine and eat raw eggs, which was her diet until the end. The day she died she remained alert until I came to see her. The nurse said my mother was waiting for me. I was by her side when she passed away. This was

March 3, 1957, during my last year at the Gymnasium but before my graduation.

Shortly after my mother's passing I had my final exams. These evaluations in the Gymnasium are both written and oral. For the oral exams, the professors were exchanged with those from other Gymnasiums so that the students did not know them and no partiality could be shown. These were particularly difficult. The students remained in the classroom and a panel of professors from all disciplines came in. Each student was then called upon for his oral exam. He would not know which professor or subject he would be asked about. The entire class watched. I was initially quizzed pretty thoroughly on literature that I had not read. Fortunately, another professor began questioning me on subjects I did know such as physics, chemistry and math. The written exams were like a typical classroom test except the papers were sent away to be evaluated by professors other than those who had actually taught the subject. I passed both the written and oral exams. I graduated from the Gymnasium on March 30, 1957, at the age of twenty-one. I was three years behind because of all the moving, restarting first grade and the war.

CHAPTER 24

Going Home

Riding a bicycle has always been a part of my life. The only exceptions were while in Crystal City and after my bicycle was bartered in Steinkirchen. My dad bought me a nice new bicycle after we moved to Konstanz.

Because I was an American citizen, occasionally I had to visit the Consulate in Stuttgart. They wanted to know how I was doing and what activities I was involved in. They inquired about how I was doing in school. I went there twice while we lived in Konstanz. Each time I rode my bicycle. It took me two days over mountainous terrain. Instead of rim brakes, the bike had torpedo brakes in the rear axle that could easily overheat if used too much on downhill runs. In an effort to avoid this problem I often was freewheeling and going way too fast for the sharp curves. This made for an exciting and dangerous ride on those mountainous roads with no guardrails along the side. After my visit I had to make the two-day return trip. My overnight stays each way were in youth hostels.

In 1957 the Consulate suggested that I could return to the US to maintain my citizenship. I had already made up my mind that I wanted to go back to America, but first I had to earn the money for my passage.

Without making a career commitment, the only available jobs around Konstanz were low-paying. I took whatever I could get. I dug ditches and I hauled bricks for masons. I worked and saved all I could until I had about half the money I needed for the fare. I then borrowed some money from two friends. They both trusted me enough to loan me the money and let me go off to another country.

I purchased my ticket on the Holland America Line. It was the lowest class passage in the belly of the ship. It cost about 800 Deutch Marks which was about $200. As it turned out, I would pay my friends back promptly out of my basic pay as an Airman Third Class in the United States Air Force.

I took the train to Holland and on January 24, 1958, I departed Rotterdam for the US aboard the SS Ryndam!

PART TWO

CHAPTER 25

Basic Training — Photography School

At Whitehall in New York City, I had at least managed to get myself signed up for the Air Force. At some point I discovered I had signed up for four years. I was really alright with that though, because I reasoned that four years would give me time to get a better feel for things in the US and to learn how I might fit in. Additionally, I still hoped that I could learn to fly and even to go to Florida.

First I was sent directly to Lackland Air Force Base for Basic Training. There I was, back in Texas, in San Antonio, just about a hundred miles north of Crystal City! The first thing the Training Instructor (TI) did when we were assigned to barracks was a shakedown. We had to empty our belongings onto our bunk and the TI went through everything. In that process I lost my Boy Scout hunting knives. Supposedly they were safe guarded and would be returned at the end of training, but I never saw them again. These were my favorite knives in handmade scabbards. I treasured those knives and regret that I lost them.

When graduation and assignment time approached, for some reason they did not have an assignment for me. I have no idea why. They finally told me I would go to the next school that opened up no matter what it was. That would determine what I was going to be in the Air Force. I knew I wasn't going to pilot training but I hoped it would at least be in Florida.

Finally I got an assignment to Still Photography School at Lowry Air Force Base in Denver, Colorado, home of the new Air Force Academy. The training was fourteen weeks long and included photography and darkroom procedures, as well as aerial photography film processing and printing.

At Lowry we slept in open bay barracks that had to always be inspection-ready. One time I had the misfortune of falling asleep leaving my locker open. The First Sergeant came through checking things and found my area and me not inspection-ready. This was not a good day!

I had made a new friend who suggested that I do as he did. Through a local church he had made friends with an older couple who did not have any children. They seemed to have a need, probably a holdover from World War II, to provide for the young military men. My friend's area was always inspection-ready because he stayed with that couple during off-duty time. He suggested that I, too, could stay with them, which I did. I never had an inspection problem again; everything was left in pristine order. My friend had an old Oldsmobile which was our transportation back and forth from the base to the older couple's home.

The two of us attended church with the couple. I had never been in a church like this. The teaching was

Bible-based and encouraged people to search scriptures on their own to determine their meaning. My previous church experience was more based on instruction from the pulpit rather than individual Bible study. I liked the idea that I was encouraged to read the Bible and interpret the Scriptures myself rather than being told what they mean.

The older couple, in that short time, became like family. We could see that they were really living their Christian faith. They fed us, took us horseback riding and showed us many interesting places. They even bought me a 1949 Ford. I drove that car even though I did not have a license. I often packed it full of other young people from church and went for a picnic or something fun.

The older couple that "adopted" us had a farm outside of town and we "helped" them there from time to time. We thought what we were doing was helping but we were more of a two-man wrecking crew. We did not know anything about anything we were doing. The sheetrock we hung in the farmhouse looked like a jigsaw puzzle. We accidentally cut down a row of fence posts and wrecked their Farmall tractor by driving it into their brand-new Plymouth. They never seemed to mind or be upset in any way.

One time my friend had to go home to New York to take care of some business and I planned to go with him. The older couple did not think we could make it in my friend's old car. They insisted we take their brand-new Plymouth and leave the old Oldsmobile for them to drive. We had to make a quick trip and I had to help with the driving even though we did not know if I could even drive that car. I sat next to my friend on the right side and drove from there while he slept with his head back on the seat and his right arm thrown back over the seat behind me.

One time while I was driving, we were on a two-lane curved road which made it difficult for me to stay in my lane. A police car going in the opposite direction saw something was not quite right and turned his cruiser right around. I quickly woke my friend and since he, of course, had a valid driver's license, the policeman let us go. Maybe he doubted what he had seen.

During that short time in Colorado my friend and I learned some valuable things from the older couple. They were true Americans who really felt a duty to those service "boys" that were stationed near them. But they also were great examples as Christians. They loved the Lord, were so willing to share anything the Lord had given them and were joyful in whatever came their way. I have included this experience because of the profound effect they had on my life and my Christian journey. While we were with them we learned a little bit about farming and a whole lot about what it means to really be a Christian. I stayed in touch with them for many years until they passed away.

CHAPTER 26

My Enlisted Years

In the Air Force we had what we called a "dream sheet," which was a form we filled out indicating where we wanted to go and what we wanted to do. Supposedly this was used when it was time for a new assignment. We all knew it did not seem to have any influence whatsoever. "The needs of the military come first." I had, of course, put on my dream sheet that I wanted to fly and wanted to go to Florida.

When I finished my training in Colorado and got my new assignment, it was not to flight school or to

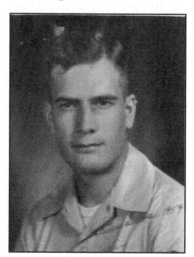

Airman Wesselhoeft (Second Class), Yokota AFB, Japan

Florida; it was to Yokota, JAPAN! I had been in the States less than a year and I suppose my English had improved a bit, but here I was going to Japan. I would hardly be able to communicate with anyone there! And so much for having the time to learn about the US and ways I might fit in. In a lucky break, my friend also got the same assignment. So off we went to Yokota Air Force Base, Japan. We found a church near the base and made some lifelong friends there. I continued to study and grow in the Word of God. I also attended a retreat, The Far East Fellowship, in Tokyo during which time we did a lot of Bible study and I got to hear the president of Pepperdine College speak. Attending The Far East Fellowship was actually supported by the military. We could have time off to attend without having to take personal leave. Military people came from all over the Pacific theater to attend. I also visited Ibaraki Christian College located north of Tokyo. I was told that during the war Ibaraki was shelled by mistake and the people asked that a Christian college be built there. While in Japan I got to meet and know many missionaries. Through all of these experiences I was able to grow as a Christian and build on the simple belief in God that I had had from an early age.

One night when I was standing on the flightline on guard duty for airplanes, I was meditating on scriptures I had been studying recently. Ephesians 4:5 kept coming to my mind. "One Lord, one faith, one baptism." (KJV)

I continued to study the Bible independently and came to Matthew 28:18-20 which says, "Then Jesus came to them and said, 'All power is given unto me in heaven and in earth. Go ye therefore, and teach all nations, baptizing them in the name of the Father, and of the Son, and of the Holy Ghost; teaching them to observe all things whatsoever I have commanded you; and, lo, I am with you always, even unto the very end of the world.'" (KJV)

Also examples in the book of Acts of the Apostles taught me that each person who became a Christian was baptized. I made the decision and was baptized at the Far East Fellowship in Tokyo, Japan, in 1959.

While in Japan, I applied again for pilot training through the Air Force. In the meantime, I decided to learn to fly on my own. For $5 an hour I could get the

Wes learning to fly at Yokota, Japan

airplane, fuel, and the mechanic. I took lessons and soloed.

Then I decided that having seen a bit of Japan from the air, I would buy a motorcycle and see it from the ground. I bought a BSA Super Rocket. I rode that motorcycle many miles in Japan.

When my tour was nearing the end I again put on my "dream sheet" that I wanted to go to pilot training and to Florida. My assignment came and it was to Dayton, Ohio, to help photograph and file logistical information.

Because of my low rank and time in service I had no allowance for sending a vehicle to the States. However I figured out that I could ship my motorcycle through the postal system. The overseas military mail is all shipped through an APO or FPO at an entry/exit point in the US. This meant that military personnel could ship and receive packages while overseas with the postage calculated between the APO/FPO and the stateside address. This was considerably less expensive than it would cost to ship a package through the local postal system in a foreign country to an address in the US. In our case we used the APO in San Francisco. The package could not exceed fifty pounds. So I took the motorcycle apart, cut the frame, packed it in boxes and shipped it via the APO to friends who lived near San Francisco. The postage was only for the short distance from San Francisco to their home. The motorcycle weighed somewhere around 500 pounds and required about twelve boxes. The postage was only a few dollars per box. My friend reassembled the motorcycle for me. He also enjoyed riding it while it was with him.

Wes on BSA motorcycle Yokota, Japan

In Ohio, I was told that the Air Force did not need pilots but that I could apply for navigator training and after that, for pilot training. Supposedly my chance to get in pilot training would be improved by having navigator training. I applied and was accepted. I went to California, picked up my motorcycle and rode it to my new assignment as a navigator trainee.

CHAPTER 27

Finally Flying

In June 1961, I arrived back in Texas assigned to Harlingen Air Force Base in the far south valley of the Rio Grande for Aviation Cadet Training. In this program, I received navigator training and became a commissioned officer at the same time. I graduated in 1962.

Now a second lieutenant, I was still trying to get into pilot training. I was told that they needed

Second Lieutenant Wesselhoeft

Electronic Warfare Officers and I should go to that school first. I was sent to Mather Air Force Base in California for Electronic Warfare Officer (EWO) training. I still struggled a bit with the English language but finished as a Distinguished Graduate. Ultimately, I was too old to go to pilot training in the Air Force.

Looking back I believe that I was better suited as an Electronic Warfare Officer. I had a good foundation in electronics from courses I had taken through the city in Konstanz. This prepared me well for the EWO training I received in the Air Force. I enjoyed the intellectual challenge of trying to stay a step ahead of our enemy and was proud of the skills and equipment I had. I was honored to have that role in keeping our crew safe and accomplishing our mission.

I served twice in Vietnam. The first was a one-year tour of duty in 1968, the year of the Tet Offensive, when I was stationed at Korat Royal Thai Air Field, flying in the EC121R. We were a flying command post monitoring the McNamara Fence. This was a brilliant strategy whereby we could monitor the movement of any equipment by our enemy along the Ho Chi Minh Trail. We could even detect bicycles. The equipment was also able to pick up conversations. From our position in the airplane we could call in immediate air strikes on troops and supplies being moved. This was an ingenious and very effective plan. During my tour I also had the rare opportunity to serve as a military liaison escort officer for a USO group traveling to Army Ranger camps in Southeast Asia.

In 1969 my father passed away and I was unable to attend his funeral. He had continued to live in Konstanz. After returning to the US in 1958 I began writing to the State Department hoping to get per-

Wes as Electronic Warfare Officer in B-52D

mission for him to come to visit me. Finally I got permission but by then he was too old. He would have loved to have come back to the US, meet my family and learn about the life I had made here.

On my second combat assignment I spent the last six months of 1972 in Vietnam flying B-52Ds from Guam and U-Tapao Royal Thai Navy Airfield. This operation was called Linebacker I. Ironically, during that time I was under the command of the Eighth Air Force, the famous "Mighty Eighth" that had bombed Hamburg during World War II.

One of the B-52s I flew in the combat area is now at the Barksdale Global Power Museum on Barksdale Air Force Base, near Bossier City, Louisiana.

I finished out my Air Force flying career as an EWO in the nuclear version B-52H at Wurtsmith AFB, Michigan. I never got that assignment to Florida but did set foot in Florida twice, once on a cross-country flight during navigator training and again when I went to water survival school in 1974.

I served twenty-two years in the Air Force and accumulated a total of 5525 flying hours; 1230 of those were in combat. I retired in 1980 as a lieutenant colonel.

Years earlier while still living in Germany, I had made plans to go around the world with one of my buddies from the Norway trip. Our intention was to go together, but instead I got an opportunity to come to America and took it. During my twenty-two years in the Air Force, I think I can safely say I went around the world. My friend also went around the world on his own. He took whatever transportation he could get, stopped to work when he needed money and then moved on. Much like our leapfrog trip to Norway, we traveled independently but actually met up in Japan and again in San Antonio. We both accomplished our mission.

Wes at Vietnam Welcome Home event, Bossier City, Louisiana, held on November 11, 2016

CHAPTER 28

Life After the Air Force

During my career in the Air Force I applied for and was accepted to the Air Force Institute of Technology to go to the University of Missouri to get my degree in Electrical Engineering. The Air Force only allowed me two years to complete the degree. I already had some college credits but not in that field. I took about 20 credit hours per semester and graduated cum laude in June 1971.

After retiring from the Air Force I wanted to work as an engineer in Civil Service. However, there is a mandatory one-year waiting period after retiring from the military. I had learned to sail and owned a nice boat. During that year I operated a charter business on Lake Huron. I had been well prepared for this during my service in the Coast Guard Auxiliary on Lake Huron from 1977 to 1991, during which I conducted safety courses for the public and inspected their boats and equipment. I also was involved in search and rescue operations on the lake.

In my free time I still wanted to enjoy my hobby of cycling. I had sold my BSA motorcycle several years earlier so I bought a Harley-Davidson which I kept for several years. I also had a Schwinn touring bicycle that I rode along the coast of Lake Huron, sometimes riding fifty or more miles.

After one year I went to work for Civil Service. I worked for the Department of Defense at Wurtsmith AFB until 1991. I spent the remainder of my working years as a Professional Engineer in the Department

Wes just after being partnered with his new guide dog, Nealy, 2015

of Energy with the Strategic Petroleum Reserve (SPR) on the Gulf Coast. During my employment with the SPR I once again encountered the indestructible German ersatz rubber, Buna. Today seals are made of it for use in the petroleum industry. I retired from Civil Service in January 2006. My entire career life, forty-eight years, was spent working for the United States Government.

Like many Vietnam veterans, I later developed some health problems related to Agent Orange exposure. I have had two bouts with non-Hodgkin's lymphoma and have been left legally blind as a result. I have no vision in my right eye, have limited pencil vision in the left, and I do not see color. I have had extremely high spinal pressure and as a result have a shunt implanted in my head. I have lost almost all my hearing. I am a 100% Service Connected Disabled Veteran. I travel with my trusted guide dog, Nealy.

I still continue my Bible study. The Veterans Administration has provided me with a text-to-voice computer program which I have used to write a Bible study guide which is now on Amazon as an ebook. They also provided me with an iPhone and a Bluetooth device connected to my hearing aides. This allows me to listen to Scriptures anytime. I have "read" through the Bible many times using this equipment.

Even without my vision I still ride a bicycle. I have all the proper equipment and have been trained by Olympians to ride on the back seat of a tandem racing bike. I take every opportunity I can find to race. Actually, I do just about everything I did before, including woodworking. I, of course, cannot drive a car, but that day may be coming.

Wild West postcard from Crystal City shop

CHAPTER 29

Conclusion

I lived in the United States until age seven. During those years America made an indelible imprint on my life. I knew what it was to be carefree and happy while living in Chicago. I had enjoyed a friendly, safe neighborhood and loved going to the beach with my family. Even in Crystal City being held behind a barbed-wire fence, I was still being influenced in a positive way by America. I had to go to the German School but I do not remember anything I learned there.

But I sure do remember the treasures I bought in the little store on the camp. The cowboy cards that I purchased represented American freedom at its best. What could be more free than a cowboy out on the wide-open range, sleeping by a campfire under the stars at night. The science fiction books that I enjoyed so much also made an important impression on me. The superheroes were American heroes who were always fighting for what was right and always winning. The futuristic devices that they used such as rockets and talking watches inspired me to believe that the future would be in America. This is where those things would be invented and would be used for good. I never forgot the impression that America had upon me.

From a very early age, at least by four when I survived a ruptured appendix, I knew that there is a God. I somehow always trusted that God exists. During the war years and the awful years following, life was very hard. I just had to trust God day by day. We never knew what the next day would bring. Would our home be bombed out, would we have enough food to eat, would we be warm enough, or would we even all be alive?

I still believe that there is a God and that He is in charge. He gives us guidance through his word, the Bible. He would not have given us the Bible had He not intended us to use it. I learned along the way that I needed to be responsible for my understanding of the Scriptures. I, of course, learned much from preachers, teachers and the example of others, but ultimately I must reach my own understanding and develop my own faith.

I have always trusted that God knows what is best. Even the day I walked into the recruiting office at Times Square, alone and with only ten dollars in my pocket, I was certain everything would be ok.

I sometimes had my own ideas of what should happen and in many cases things did not work out as I thought they should. As a little child who loved airplanes it was a perfectly natural thing to think I should be a pilot. After all, I did not know what anyone else might do in an airplane. But I believe the best thing happened to me when I became an Electronic Warfare Officer. I excelled in that position and think I would not have excelled as a pilot.

Today I am in remission from non-Hodgkin's lymphoma but am legally blind. I still take each day as it comes because I do not know what the Lord has in mind.

I am honored to have served for over twenty-two years in the United States Air Force and to have retired at the rank of lieutenant colonel. I am also proud of my more than twenty-five years in Civil Service. I served my country for a total of almost forty-eight years.

In recent years I learned that I was exchanged for other Americans, some of whom were wounded soldiers, diplomats and Americans trapped behind enemy lines when World War II broke out. I am proud that I actually began serving my beloved country when I was six, interned and traded for these Americans. I find comfort in knowing that my family's suffering helped other families.

But they that wait upon the Lord shall renew their strength; they shall mount up with wings of eagles; they shall run, and not be weary, and they shall walk, and not faint. Isaiah 40:31 KJV

Addendum

I have learned that Japanese Americans and Italian Americans who were interned during World War II have been recognized by our government. However, the internment of German Americans has not, as of this writing, been recognized. I respectfully request Congressional and Presidential recognition of the internment as well as the exchange of German Americans with our enemy, many of whom were American citizens. I would like our government to take actions to educate Americans about the internment and trade of German Americans. I would like our internment to be included on any markers at interment sites where German Americans were held. I am not asking for an apology or reparations even though others have received them.

I believe it is time to make peace with this part of our American history and to acknowledge and learn the full story of World War II internment.

75th Anniversary

March 25, 2018, was the seventy-fifth anniversary of my internment in Crystal City, Texas. To commemorate I had the honor of family, friends, and dignitaries gathering at the site to recognize this significant event in my life. I was a six-year-old American boy when my family was taken from Chicago under armed guard and placed behind barbed wire fences in a faraway place called Crystal City.

Each family member who was present had a part in our ceremony. My wife, Shirley, presented me with a flag that had flown over the Capitol in Washington, DC. She also had made arrangements for a flag to be flown in my honor over the Capitol on March 25, 2018, in recognition of the anniversary of my internment at Crystal City.

Following the ceremony many of us toured the grounds of the former internment camp. Of course, this time there were no barbed-wire fences, no armed guards and no internees. We were told that the only remaining building is the German school. Of course this was an important stop for us. The swimming pool is still easily recognizable although the concrete is broken and showing its age. The Texas Historical Commission (THC) has placed signage at various locations around the site. We are very grateful for their diligence in studying the history of the site and placing signage. If it were not for THC I know of nothing that would indicate any German Americans were ever held there.

After returning home we learned that Crystal City Family Internment Camp is actually on the National Register of Historic Places. We have the document from the Department of Interior which tells of the many German Americans who were actually the first occupants. Throughout the camp's existence it held German American internees.

With this being the seventy-fifth anniversary, we decided to travel to the locations that were significant in my internment, exchange, and return to America. I was certain that things had changed in the sixty and seventy-five years that had passed since I was in New York and Chicago respectively. But, I thought I would at least see places I remembered, that it would be a bit of a nostalgia trip. Surely there would be some historical notation of those places that were significant to the history of our country.

In late May we traveled by car to Washington, DC, for Memorial Day. We visited the American Veterans Disabled for Life Memorial which is absolutely beautiful. Of course we paid our respects at the Vietnam Memorial and the World War II Memorial. We were also able to enjoy the Rolling Thunder parade as well as a patriotic concert at the Kennedy Center.

After Memorial Day we took the train to New York where we met Shirley's daughter, Heather Spillers. We visited all the significant places—Times Square, the recruiting office, 39 Whitehall Street, Governor's Island, and Hoboken where I had returned to the US.

In Hoboken, New Jersey, we went to the Hoboken Memorial Museum and the wonderful people there were very helpful. We learned about things that pertain to my personal history of having arrived in Hoboken but also that the little town had played a very big role in World War I.

The *Ryndam* on which I arrived docked at the 5th Street Pier on February 3, 1958. The Holland America Line no longer docks in Hoboken and the pier is gone, but at the museum we learned exactly where the pier had been and were able to go there to take pictures. It is a pretty area with a soccer field and a small restaurant. But sadly, nothing there indicates the history of the location except that when the piers were removed, the city took the bollards from the docks and placed them along the edge of the sidewalks, really quite an attractive effect. But it left me with a bit of a sad feeling. Yes, it is a very pretty place to visit but there is no indication of its significance in American history, not only as a port of entry but particularly its role in World War I.

From Hoboken we took a bus to Times Square as I had done in 1958. Times Square is still just a sea of moving people, moving vehicles and moving lights. We even stopped at a hot dog stand. The recruiting office is still there but now it is in a new building. It looks quite different but fits right in with the look of Times Square, unmistakable with its brightly-lit

American flag on the sides and with service seals from each branch on the front. We went inside and found some things were still the same—the desks were still lined up perpendicular to the wall and while we were there, only one person came in to talk to a recruiter!

The building at 29 Whitehall looks entirely different. It is completely covered with glass and looks much like any other building in the area. In this building thousands of new recruits had lined up to be processed into the military. Many surely gave their lives for this country. Unfortunately, I saw no indication of its important place in American history. Anyone passing by would have no idea of the significance this building has played in the freedom they now enjoy.

On Governors Island we felt pretty sure we located the building where I ate and slept that second night in America. We located it based on my memory of where it was, not because there was any other indication of how this area had been used by the military in years past except for the fort itself.

The Staten Island Ferry provides an excellent view of the Statue of Liberty, about the only thing that was still recognizable and a cherished memory from my early New York experience.

We went back to Washington and spent a few days doing research in the National Archives. This is quite a daunting task especially for the newcomer. We learned from our experience that material about the internment, especially of the German Americans, is difficult to find. It seems we had to look within records of various agencies such as Immigration and Naturalization and the Justice Department. It was quite a maze to work through. The people who work there and even others who were doing research on their own topic were very helpful.

I was able to obtain one item that I particularly wanted. I now have the manifest from my voyage on the *SS Gripsholm* in February 1944. Now I would like to get the manifest of the return voyage. I am very interested in knowing for whom we were exchanged. We hope to go back again.

It was disappointing that finding material on German internment in World War II was so difficult. It is a fact that German Americans were interned and were traded with our enemy, Nazi Germany. Somewhere that agreement must exist. This is another document I would like to find. I think that our government should make this part of our history easier to research.

From Washington we took a side trip to Fort McHenry where the national anthem was written by Francis Scott Key. This actually turned out to be one of the highlights of our trip. Of course the birth of *The Star-Spangled Banner* ranks among some of the most important events in our history. And the government has done a beautiful job of telling the story. We know that other events do not rise to that level but need to be recognized and known by our people nevertheless.

Someone had asked how I felt about my service in Vietnam after I had experienced the bombings by the Allies. My answer was simple—they were our enemies. While we were at Fort McHenry, I told my wife that if I had been there at that time I would have fought the British because they were the enemy.

We had contacted the Mennonite Central Committee in Akron, Pennsylvania, before we left home. They had sent the little book of Christmas hymns to internees at Crystal City and it is the only thing I remember from my Christmas in the camp. We made a photocopy of the booklet, took it to them and were able to express our appreciation even some seventy-five years later.

For someone who had always had an interest in airplanes the National Museum of the US Air Force in Dayton, Ohio, was a must-see. It is the oldest and largest aviation museum in the world with a wonderful collection of aircraft spanning the history of flight. We were even able to go inside an Air Force One! I would have liked to have seen a display of the EC121R and exhibit on the McNamara Fence that was such an ingenious strategy in Vietnam.

From there we went on to Chicago. While we could have driven to my boyhood home on Kenmore Avenue we decided to walk the more than two miles from our hotel. It was a pleasant, tree-lined street. On the way we stopped in a little shop for a snack and the people were so friendly and helpful. They pointed out the Edgewater Hotel which was an important landmark for me. Finally, we reached the apartment complex my parents had managed and where I had lived before we were taken away to Crystal City. Of course, alterations to the building made it unrecognizable to me, including a new metal fence around it. We walked around back where I had ridden my bicycle as a free little boy.

It was only a short walk over to the Goudy School that I had attended as a first-grader. The school was just as it had been with few exceptions. The long building had been added on to either end but the original building was exactly like it was in 1943 when I attended. We were able to go inside and while I could not remember where my room had been, I was very pleased to see that the school had not been renovated. Original wooden doors showed hand marks resulting from many years of touching. The auditorium stage had wooden panels that folded open rather than a curtain. We took many pictures inside. Again, everyone was nice and accommodating.

My parents and I often walked down to the beach and we have pictures that have the Edgewater Hotel in the background. We were not sure exactly the route my family might have taken but we decided to take what seemed like a route that would get us there given the changes in the streets between Kenmore Avenue and the beach area. We were very fortunate that we came out on the beach area right where my parents had taken a picture of me. Now we have that picture and a picture of me at age eighty-one standing in just about the same place. We walked along the beach where I had played with my parents when I lived in Chicago. We also just sat on a bench and enjoyed the pleasant breeze from the lake. It was so nice to be in this place that had not changed. The beach was still there, the concrete where I had stood and the Edgewater Hotel was still in the background. This place was real as were all the other places. But those places were changed and for the most part unrecognized.

Even my guide dog, Nealy, seemed to have a nostalgic moment. He had spent his first year of training with a couple who live on the northern California coast and he had play time at the beach. It is the first beach he has been to since then and he loved it!

The following day we went to the big Victorian home on Ellis Avenue, a home that was used to house "enemy alien" men. I, of course, did not know at the time that my dad was being held there. No passerby today would have any idea it had once been used to detain "enemy aliens."

Our last stop in Chicago was at the Norwegian American Hospital where I was born an American citizen on September 8, 1936. It is also the hospital where I had been taken with a ruptured appendix when I was four.

In our travels we found everyone to be friendly, polite and helpful. Everywhere we went people came up to me and thanked me for my service.

In September Shirley and I took the final leg of our remembrance trip. We went with some family members to visit Hamburg and Steinkirchen where I had lived during the War.

We had the good fortune to visit Steinkirchen on a day when they were having an Apple Festival. Visiting the small village was even more fun because of the music, food and dancing. The dancers all wore their traditional costumes which are quite different from those that most people think of as German such as Lederhosen.

We were able to easily locate the home I had lived in with my parents and grandparents. There were some changes to it, of course. The ditches along the sides and the front that had so fascinated me as a little boy were no longer there. The room upstairs that I shared with my mother now has a skylight. I was able to locate the grain mill, which is still standing and is now an apartment building. I pointed out where my friends and I had gotten a tow on our sleds from cars moving by. It seems they enjoyed imagining those boys and their play.

Much like candy bars today just aren't as big as they were when we were youngsters, the river is just not as big as it was when I was young. It is still navigable by fairly large boats, however, and the extremes of depth caused by the tides coming in and out are still evident.

Steinkirchen today is a picturesque village and the entire area known as *Das Alte Land* (The Old Land) attracts many tourists.

In Hamburg our primary interest was St. Nicholas Church. The city has been rebuilt so that it looks as if it had not been destroyed. However, the Church was left in its bombed-out state. Only the spire remains. We took an elevator to the top and were able to have a 360-degree view of the city and its huge harbor.

In a basement area below the spire a museum tells the sad story of the destruction of the city. The account was a very fair history and even pointed out that England has suffered similar destruction from the Third Reich. A small youth orchestra was practicing in a side area and their beautiful classical music added to the ambiance of the museum. As we were leaving we noticed that people had gathered in the courtyard to listen to the bells that would soon be chiming.

We have added some pictures that we took in Steinkirchen and in Hamburg.

After our trip to Germany we made a another quick trip to Washington, DC. We were there to hear a speech by our congressman, Dr. Ralph Abraham. We sat in the gallery of the United States House of Representatives while Dr. Abraham gave a brief overview of my life and career. There are just no words to express how it felt to be sitting in the gallery and hearing our congressman honor me in such a way. I am humbled and deeply grateful.

Dr. Abraham's speech can be found on YouTube: https://www.youtube.com/watch?v=NMZ9HTZ5bOA

On or about February 15, 2019, we plan to have another commemoration in remembrance of my family being taken from Crystal City again under armed guard to board the *SS Gripsholm*. The ship took us to Lisbon, Portugal, where we were traded with our enemy and sent into the active war zone.

Impressions I have now that I have been back is that I regret that we Americans do not honor our history as much as we could. We are very innovative people and are always moving forward and of course things change over time. But all the important things that happened to me and my family pertaining to internment, exchange and even my return and enlistment are almost as if they never even happened.

This is part of American history. We Americans have not always done the right thing, but one thing that makes us exceptional is that from time to time we have recognized where we were wrong and have made efforts to correct our course. I believe this is what needs to happen regarding German American internment and exchange.

While we were traveling and visiting sites we told everyone who would listen what had happened to me and my family. Almost no one knew that German Americans had been interned during World War II. They were usually very surprised to learn that it had happened and that somehow they had never heard of it. Most people were absolutely appalled that German Americans, many of whom were American citizens, were traded with our enemy, Nazi Germany, into the active war zone.

Many told us that my story is one that must be told, that Americans need to know about this history that they are not taught in school. But when we told them that I had returned at my earliest opportunity, had gone right away to the recruiting office at Times Square, joined the Air Force and served for twenty-two years there was typically, in one way or another, a big "Oh WOW!" Some even seemed to swell with American Pride as if they were thinking, "Yeah! That's what Americans are made of!"

The photos in this section were taken during our 75th Anniversary trip in 2018, unless otherwise noted.

75th Anniversary
Commemoration Tour

2018

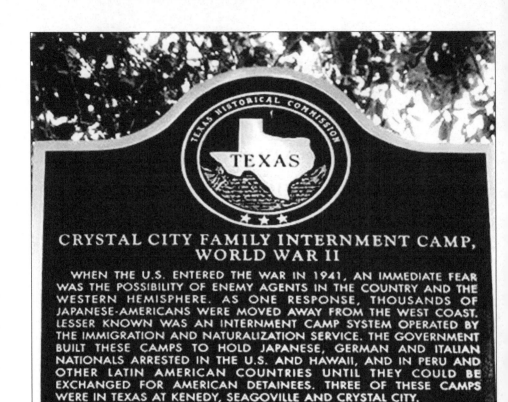

CRYSTAL CITY FAMILY INTERNMENT CAMP, WORLD WAR II

WHEN THE U.S. ENTERED THE WAR IN 1941, AN IMMEDIATE FEAR WAS THE POSSIBILITY OF ENEMY AGENTS IN THE COUNTRY AND THE WESTERN HEMISPHERE. AS ONE RESPONSE, THOUSANDS OF JAPANESE-AMERICANS WERE MOVED AWAY FROM THE WEST COAST. LESSER KNOWN WAS AN INTERNMENT CAMP SYSTEM OPERATED BY THE IMMIGRATION AND NATURALIZATION SERVICE. THE GOVERNMENT BUILT THESE CAMPS TO HOLD JAPANESE, GERMAN AND ITALIAN NATIONALS ARRESTED IN THE U.S. AND HAWAII, AND IN PERU AND OTHER LATIN AMERICAN COUNTRIES UNTIL THEY COULD BE EXCHANGED FOR AMERICAN DETAINEES. THREE OF THESE CAMPS WERE IN TEXAS AT KENEDY, SEAGOVILLE AND CRYSTAL CITY.

THE CRYSTAL CITY CAMP, CONVERTED FROM AN EXISTING MIGRATORY LABOR CAMP, WAS THE LARGEST INTERNMENT FACILITY IN THE U.S. AND THE ONLY ONE BUILT EXCLUSIVELY FOR FAMILIES. THE ORIGINAL 200-ACRE CAMP LATER EXPANDED TO ALMOST 500 ACRES, WITH AGRICULTURAL AREAS AND SUPPORT FACILITIES. THE PRIMARY LIVING AREA WAS A 100-ACRE COMPOUND ENCLOSED BY A 10-FOOT BARBED WIRE FENCE, COMPLETE WITH GUARD TOWERS AND SPOTLIGHTS. LIKE A SMALL TOWN, THE COMPOUND HAD 700 BUILDINGS AND INCLUDED FAMILY HOUSING, SCHOOLS, A HOSPITAL, SHOPS, WAREHOUSES, MARKETS AND RECREATION AREAS.

ALTHOUGH INTENDED FOR JAPANESE, THE CRYSTAL CITY CAMP ALSO HELD GERMANS AND A FEW ITALIANS. THE POPULATION AVERAGED 2,800 THROUGHOUT THE WAR. IT REACHED A PEAK OF ALMOST 3,400 IN DECEMBER 1944, TWO-THIRDS OF WHOM WERE JAPANESE. AT THE END OF THE WAR, THE GOVERNMENT PAROLED INTERNEES THROUGHOUT THE U.S. OR SENT THEM TO THEIR HOME COUNTRIES. THE CRYSTAL CITY CAMP WAS THE ONLY ONE STILL IN OPERATION BY JUNE 1946. IT OFFICIALLY CLOSED FEBRUARY 27, 1948, AND THE PROPERTY TRANSFERRED TO THE CITY AND SCHOOL DISTRICT.

TEXAS IN WORLD WAR II, Y-40
(2005)

Crystal City, Texas. Sign placed at Crystal City Internment Camp site by the Texas Historical Commission

Crystal City. Wes, Nealy and Statue of Popeye

In Chicago, Wes read Popeye comics and saw him as a hero. Then he found him in Crystal City right there by the Internment Camp like a superhero protector. Crystal City, Popeye and the Wesselhoefts were all innocently thrown into the middle of World War II.

Crystal City. Wes and Nealy at site of the swimming pool, now broken and covered with vegetation

Hoboken, New Jersey. In retracing Wes' history, we also learned that Hoboken was an important port in World War I.

Hoboken Museum staff told us where to find the original pier where the *Ryndam* returned Wes to the US.

Hoboken. The pier where the *Ryndam* docked in 1958, where Wes took his first step onto American soil as he returned to the US

Hoboken. Wes and Heather enjoying a snack at a restaurant built on the site through which Wes processed when he entered as an American citizen in 1958

New York City. Another hot dog at a Times Square stand

New York City. Times Square Recruiting Office, 2018

New York City. Wes at Times Square Recruiting Office, 2018 *Some things never change…you wait.*

Fort Jay, Governors Island. Wes believes this is the building where he spent his second night in America after returning

New York City. The building at 39 Whitehall Street did not show a sign of its historical significance in 2018.

New York. From the ferry

Wes with his limited vision trying to see the Statue of Liberty and remembering

Akron, Pennsylvania. Visit to Mennonite Central Committee, in thanks for the hymn book. Even that small gesture was memorable, the only thing Wes remembers from that Christmas.

Chicago, Illinois. At the house on Kenmore Avenue, Wes longed to go inside and see the apartment he shared with his mother and father when he was a boy.

Chicago. Goudy School, where Wes went to first grade, where every day he stood, placed his hand over his heart and said the Pledge of Allegiance

Chicago. Wes and Nealy on a spot very close to where Wes' picture had been taken when he was a little boy

Chicago. On the beach, still watching airplanes every chance he gets….

Chicago. House on Ellis Avenue where Wes' father was held. There is nothing to indicate its role in American history.

Wes remembers his own flying experience & his experience during World War II

Shreveport, Louisiana. Wes after flying in a B-17. He got a sense of what the crews were experiencing in the air while he was enduring its wrath in Hamburg during World War II.

Barksdale AFB, Louisiana. Wes and Nealy by a B-52D ("BUFF") that he flew in combat. This aircraft is now on static display at the Barksdale Global Power Museum. Red bomb symbols indicate the number of bombing missions.

Washington, DC. Wes at Vietnam Memorial on Memorial Day, 2018

Steinkirchen. House where Wes lived with this parents and grandparents during the war, as it looks today.

Stade. Athenaeum Gymnasium in Stade which Wes attended 1948–50

Steinkirchen. Dancers in traditional costumes at Apple Festival

Steinkirchen.
Wes with the
Queen of the
Apple Festival

A Tale of Two Spires

Steinkirchen. Church in Steinkirchen after which the town was named, spared in World War II

Hamburg. Remaining spire of bombed-out, burned-out St. Nicholas Church, deliberately left as a reminder of the cost of war

Hamburg. Air raid victims being buried in mass graves. Photo of exhibit at St. Nicholas Church museum

Hamburg. View of Hamburg's Old Town from the spire of St. Nicholas, 1951. Photo of exhibit at St. Nicholas Church museum

Hamburg. Statue in St. Nicholas Church

Made in the USA
Columbia, SC
23 May 2021